VALUE CLARIFICATION IN THE CLASSROOM: A PRIMER

From *To Speak or Not to Speak*, page 15

VALUE CLARIFICATION IN THE CLASSROOM: A PRIMER

J. DOYLE CASTEEL
UNIVERSITY OF FLORIDA, GAINESVILLE
ROBERT J. STAHL
MISSISSIPPI UNIVERSITY FOR WOMEN

Goodyear Publishing Company, Inc., Santa Monica, California

From *A Mental Case or Two*, page 91

From *Company Man*, page 129

From *Ode to the Jailbird*, page 97

For

Peggy Jo, Sherry, Jimmy,
and "Little Bit" Casteel

and

Barbie and Stevie Stahl

Current printing (last digit):
10 9 8 7 6 5 4 3 2

ISBN: 0-87620-940-1

Library of Congress Catalog Card Number: 74-9046

Y-9401-4

Cover and Interior Design by John Isely

Printed in the United States of America

CONTENTS

GOODYEAR EDUCATION SERIES
Theodore W. Hipple, Editor

CHANGE FOR CHILDREN
Sandra Nina Kaplan, Jo Ann Butom Kaplan, Sheila Kunishima Madsen, Bette K. Taylor

CRUCIAL ISSUES IN CONTEMPORARY EDUCATION
Theodore W. Hipple

EARLY CHILDHOOD EDUCATION
Marjorie Hipple

ELEMENTARY SCHOOL TEACHING: PROBLEMS AND METHODS
Margaret Kelly Giblin

FACILITATIVE TEACHING: THEORY AND PRACTICE
Robert Myrick and Joe Wittmer

THE FOUR FACES OF TEACHING
Dorothy I. Seaberg

THE FUTURE OF EDUCATION
Theodore W. Hipple

MASTERING CLASSROOM COMMUNICATION
Dorothy Grant Hennings

THE OTHER SIDE OF THE REPORT CARD
Larry Chase

POPULAR MEDIA AND THE TEACHING OF ENGLISH
Thomas R. Giblin

RACE AND POLITICS IN SCHOOL/COMMUNITY ORGANIZATIONS
Allan C. Ornstein

REFORMING METROPOLITAN SCHOOLS
Allan Ornstein, Daniel Levine, Doxey Wilkerson

SCHOOL COUNSELING: PROBLEMS AND METHODS
Robert Hyrick and Joe Wittmer

SECONDARY SCHOOL TEACHING: PROBLEMS AND METHODS
Theodore W. Hipple

SOLVING TEACHING PROBLEMS
Mildred Bluming and Myron Dembo

TEACHING, LOVING, AND SELF-DIRECTED LEARNING
David Thatcher

VALUE CLARIFICATION IN THE CLASSROOM: A PRIMER
Doyle Casteel and Robert Stahl

WILL THE REAL TEACHER PLEASE STAND UP?
Mary Greer and Bonnie Rubinstein

SOCIAL STUDIES AS CONTROVERSY
R. Jerrald Shive

A YOUNG CHILD EXPERIENCES
Sandra Nina Kaplan, Jo Ann Butom Kaplan, Sheila Kunishima Madsen, Bette K. Taylor

PREFACE

Valuing and values are integral elements of knowing and thinking. What is worth knowing? Which procedure is best? Which authority should I believe? How will I justify my decision? These are questions with which we all wrestle as we acquire new knowledge, assign meaning to events, and interpret our personal and social experiences.

Valuing and values are integral elements of social activity. Through social activity we internalize, and become transmitters of, the norms of our society. Through social activity we receive feedback on how others perceive our judgments and decisions, and given this information, we shape and reshape our values, beliefs, and policies. Through social activity we learn to emulate the valuing procedures that produce desirable results for others.

Valuing and values are elements of personal and social activity in the world of practical affairs. We must sometimes make decisions—individually and collectively—under restricting conditions. That is, we may often lack the time, the knowledge, or even the options necessary to arrive at a good decision. Other times we may have to support the least evil of a bad set of options.

Valuing and values are *learned*; thus they may be *taught*. Students may be taught how to express their values and feelings; they may be taught how to make choices based on grounds that they can communicate to others. Students may be taught how to create options, thus increasing the range of available alternatives. They may be taught how to analyze and assign value to known or anticipated consequences. We have the opportunity to teach students principles by which they can assign value more successfully and more responsibly.

Value Clarification in the Classroom was especially designed to be used in undergraduate, graduate, and inservice teacher education courses and modules, particularly in general teaching methods courses and special methods courses in such fields as English, social studies, and science. It is intended to develop the following understandings: What do students do when value clarification is occurring; What can teachers do to facilitate student behaviors associated with value clarification; What materials and activities are likely to stimulate and channel student behaviors related to value clarification. These understandings will help teachers organize and guide instruction in the area of value clarification.

Many people have contributed to the ideas that resulted in this book. Among these we would like to thank the following:

Monte Adkison	Bob Gasche
Wanda Baker	John Gregory
Paul Becht	J. J. Koran, Jr.
Judy Collins	Dale Merkerson
Sandi Damico	Kirby Stewart
Ed Davis	Eugene Timmerman
Tom Gadsden	Eugene Todd

We wish especially to acknowledge the services of our editor, Theodore Hipple. It was he who perceived a book in a clutter of materials. The fact that he has a track record of performing such daring feats in no way detracts from our gratitude—or makes it any easier to avoid the sin of envy.

J. Doyle Casteel
Robert J. Stahl

INTRODUCTION

Those fond of characterizing an era in a single word or phrase may well call our present time "The Age of Dichotomy." Such an expression oversimplifies, of course, but even given this caveat, it contains much truth. We are, in too large a measure, a society beset by dichotomies. We live in an age of accelerating change that forces the quick decision, the hurried response, and denies us the leisure to ponder our decision, to consider its consequences, and to look at things from the other fellow's point of view. We fall victim to polarized thinking and to extreme positions.

This assertion needs little support, though it has much: the marital discords that yearly produce a record number of divorces; the cynicism about what the "little man" can do; the increasing number of mental breakdowns; the black/white confrontations; the widening generational gaps that now must include the aged among what has traditionally been the problem of parents and their adolescent children; the differing vierwpoints of the rich and the poor about matters like welfare and guaranteed annual incomes and low cost, federally funded housing. To the serious thinker it is a pessimistic assertion, one that bodes ill to the society that makes no attempts to stem the creeping social paralysis that such dichotomous thinking, if unchecked, is sure to create.

Solutions if they are to be found, lie in an awareness of the values that, consciously or unconsciously, we know support our positions and those of others. We must come to grips with our values, a task that demands that we ask and answer such questions as these: What are my values? How are they formed? How strongly do I hold to them? How are they modified? How do they square with the values others espouse?

It is heartening that the schools have begun to be active in helping students ask these kinds of questions. Value clarification is now an important part of many educational programs. Much of it, however, is happenstance, a Friday afternoon exercise or "something we get to when the really crucial stuff (e.g., the Pythagorean theorem or the impact of the Tudor kings) is completed." In short, teachers may talk more about value clarification outside their classrooms than they explore it within them.

Casteel and Stahl hope to alter this order of things. They strongly believe in the importance of value clarification activities and in the view that such activities fit easily and fruitfully into the normal domains of the traditional disciplines of English, history, science, and so forth. On both counts they are right—absolutely so: Value clarification is important. Value clarification can, and should, be part of the on-going instructional program.

The teaching strategy they have developed is the *value sheet.* Although there are other strategies, the value sheet is certainly the most likely to be productive of changes in values, in value developments, and in the habits of value development. There are several different kinds of value sheets in this book, written so that the teacher, experienced or pre-service, can use them as is, can modify them, or, most important of all, can develop his own value sheets on topics of his own choosing. Casteel and Stahl have been careful to take the teacher/reader along with them, explaining what needs to be done, how it can be done, and why it should be done if the teacher wishes to use value sheets in his classroom.

And I, like Casteel and Stahl, hope that the teacher will choose to use value sheets. The time in which we live demands such use. The lives of pupils will profit from such use. Indeed, it may not be too much of an overstatement to suggest that the healthy continuation of society is dependent upon such use.

To Casteel and Stahl, then, I say thank you for producing a book that will help teachers help pupils and, by so doing, help society. Theirs has been an important contribution, one I hope that they are as proud of as I am to have it in the Goodyear Series in Education.

Theodore W. Hipple
Editor
Goodyear Series in Education

CHAPTER ONE

VALUE CLARIFICATION: A RATIONALE

Value clarification is one of the most important responsibilities of the classroom teacher. This statement is true for those who teach such traditional academic classes as English, mathematics, science, and social studies, and it is no less true for those who teach courses associated with career education, the fine arts, or technical skills. In order to meet the obligation of helping students clarify their values, the classroom teacher must arrive at tentative answers for three questions:

- Why should I plan for, encourage, and facilitate value clarification in my classroom?
- What behaviors do my students exhibit when they are engaged in value clarification?
- What resources and materials will I use to facilitate student value clarification?

The purpose of this book is to present some answers to these questions. It is a primer for classroom teachers and for those who would become classroom teachers.

That value clarification is one of the most important goals of instruction, can be justified on a number of grounds. This chapter will identify six reasons why the classroom teacher should stress value clarification.

COMMUNICATING

Value clarification enhances the ability of students to communicate their ideas, beliefs, values, and feelings.

Value clarification activities enable students to practice and gain skill in the expression of values, feelings, ideals, and beliefs. Given the importance of communication, the classroom teacher should not avoid value clarification or treat it superficially.

The theory of value clarification presented in this book encourages students to express and examine their beliefs, values, and feelings in a social setting and to perceive such efforts to share beliefs, values, and feelings as legitimate elements of intellectual inquiry. When value clarification activities are conducted within the social setting of the classroom, students learn to express their opinions, values, and feelings more clearly to others. At the same time, students have occasion to confront opinions and beliefs that differ from their own. This interaction leads students to begin searching for the unstated assumptions on which their opinions are founded. As one effect of such practice, students' statements with regard to beliefs, values, and feelings tend to become more precise. A second effect is that those attempting to receive, understand, and interpret their classmates' messages become better listeners. In this manner, the ability of students to communicate is enhanced by value clarification. The sender improves the quality of his messages and becomes more adept at transmitting them in a social setting; the receivers become better attuned to accept and decode messages.

EMPATHIZING

Value clarification enhances the ability of students to empathize with other persons, especially those whose circumstances may differ significantly from their own.

Because people's opinions and ideals influence how they behave in social situations, one must have some understanding of, and some ability to view, the world in terms of the preferences and emotions of others. Value clarification enables students to sharpen their awareness of how others think, value, and feel. With this increased awareness students are better equipped to consider alternative opinions and values based upon the ideals and feelings that others cherish.

The value clarification theory and activities presented in this book can be used to enhance student ability to empathize. Many of the activities provide students with a role and with a set of constraints within which they must determine preferences and make decisions. In addition, follow-up questions that accompany each activity often require students to place themselves in the position of others and to analyze how such a change in status might influence their values, their ideals, their feelings, and even their actions. When students think, decide, and judge on the basis of the opinions of persons whose environments and experiences differ from their own, they have an opportunity to practice and refine their empathizing skills.

PROBLEM SOLVING

Value clarification enhances the ability of students to resolve problems as they arise.

When men and women resolve problems, their decisions have consequences that are likely to influence others as well as themselves. This means that people who are engaged in the resolution of practical problems must be willing to accept risks that would not be present in a more perfect world. Given that an uncertain future will demand citizens who are adept at, and willing to participate in, problem resolution, value clarification activities can and should stress the practical limitations these citizens will confront.

The time within which an individual or group must make a decision in order to resolve a problem is usually limited. Because of insufficient time, a full and thorough inquiry may be impossible.

The information with which a decision-making group resolves a problem may be incomplete, fragmentary, and, to some degree, inaccurate. Group members may not have sufficient time, resources, or skills to collect all the relevant information before arriving at decisions. For similar reasons, members of decision-making groups may not be able to explore fully the probable effects of alternatives before making a final decision and establishing a policy for action. Consequently, in the world of practical affairs, people often act with incomplete knowledge of problems and issues and with inadequate consideration of all the potential effects of their actions.

Practical problems requiring resolution by decision-making groups are likely to evoke the feelings and values of members. When this occurs, the feelings and values called into play become elements of the problem-solving situation that must be identified and coped with before the problem itself can be analyzed and resolved to the mutual satisfaction of group members.

The value clarification activities presented in this book are designed to help students develop skills in the making of decisions as these occur in practical, everyday affairs. Student activities frequently contain time constraints. Some activities stress the rapid identification of likely consequences of alternative policies. Still other activities elicit personal preferences and feelings from students and make these personal commitments elements of subsequent problem-solving situations. Because value clarification activities tend to simulate many of the conditions that confront members of problem-solving groups, they provide students with an opportunity to enhance their ability to resolve problems as they are likely to be encountered in the outside world.

ASSENTING AND DISSENTING

Value clarification enhances student ability to assent and dissent as a member of a social group.

In order to exercise his freedom, a person must be able to differentiate discrete elements of his society. He must be able to analyze his society if he is to identify those elements he believes are worthy of his support. To these, he assents. He must, at the same time, be able to locate those elements unworthy of his personal support. Toward these, he dissents. To the extent that a person can make such differentiations, he can respond critically to different aspects of his society. And because he can respond critically, expressing his assent and focusing his dissent, he can also commit himself to his society.

A sense of personal commitment requires the exercise of critical capabilities. When an individual has the capacity to examine his society critically, he can rationally lend his assent to those elements of his society that he perceives to be of value. Using the same critical powers, he can dissent from and attempt to eradicate or modify elements of his society that he believes are detrimental. Given the ability to use assenting and dissenting skills, a person is likely to discover and assign meanings to his individual strivings, successes, and failures in the community of other members of his society.

The value clarification theory and activities presented in this book stress helping students to differentiate elements in social situations. At times, students are required to choose a policy from among a limited set of options—none of which is ideal. At other times, students are guided to determine the negative results they must accept if they are to obtain desired consequences. Value clarification activities thus enhance the ability of students to use individual freedoms and to participate meaningfully as members of social groups. Consequently, value clarification enables students to grow in their ability to use assenting and dissenting skills.

DECISION MAKING

Value clarification enhances the ability of students to engage in decision making.

When a person is faced with choosing between at least two things that he values equally, he experiences conflict—he must choose one alternative at the cost of surrendering the other. He surrenders the benefits he would have received had he chosen differently, and he accepts negative consequences likely to occur as a result of his decision. While an individual wrestles with making his decision, he experiences *conflict* because he cannot make a completely satisfactory choice.

Once a person has made a decision, he often experiences a similar conflict: he must deal with the negative consequences (both anticipated and unanticipated) that occur as a result of the option chosen, and he may also encounter situations in which the positive consequences of the rejected option would have been desirable. In either event, he has reason to doubt and regret the wisdom of his decision. This doubt and regret following the making of a decision is called *dissonance.*

To confidently make a decision between equally valued options, a person must be able to analyze and weigh consequences. One needs to be able to identify the common features of a range of choices, that is, to discover where choices overlap to such a degree that there is little or no difference between options. He also needs to be able to frame and articulate a basis for his choice that is self-validating and that, at the same time, is adequate to make his decision appear reasonable to others whose opinion he values. Unless he learns to resolve predecision conflict and to cope with postdecision dissonance, he may refuse to acknowledge that a decision needs to be made and, in extreme cases, may argue that his freedom and skill are irrelevant. In effect, he comes to believe that fate controls his actions and determines his experiences, and he no longer perceives himself as a responsible agent in human affairs.

The value clarification theory and exercises presented in this book are germane to helping students practice skills for coping with predecision conflict and postdecision dissonance. A number of exercises are designed to communicate to students how they can analyze the positive and negative consequences of a range of choices prior to the making of a decision. Most of the activities emphasize that policies are to be selected on the basis of clearly articulated criteria. Some shift the problem of justification away from the decision itself, asking instead that students justify negative consequences likely to follow decisions. In still other instances, students are asked to hypothesize conditions in which a decision made in good faith leads to negative results and to consider how they would cope with their feelings and values in such instances. In this way, value clarification enhances student ability to engage in decision making.

PERSONAL CONSISTENCY

Value clarification enhances student ability to hold and use consistent beliefs and disbeliefs.

In order to hold and use beliefs, an individual makes a number of decisions. He decides which beliefs to hold as true and which beliefs to reject. He does so by selecting those authorities in whom he has confidence, using good or bad reasons for his selections. He also decides what he will do with new information that conflicts with his beliefs. He can choose to modify previously held beliefs in the light of new information, or he can modify and twist new information so that it will fit in with previously held opinions. He decides, too, how he will react to the beliefs held by others. He can actively search for and consider the similarities and differences between his beliefs and those held by others; or, he can choose to accept as trustworthy authorities those who believe as he does and to reject as untrustworthy those who do not believe as he does.

Value clarification exercises and activities can help students to become consistent in their beliefs. A student is more likely to be consistent if he learns to look for differences and similarities between his beliefs and values and those held by others. He is more likely to be consistent if he learns to select authorities on whom he can rely for information. He is more likely to be consistent if he learns to accept new information by altering the beliefs he already holds.

The value clarification theory and exercises presented in this book help students to develop these skills. Students are asked to search for consistency in their opinions, preferences, and ideals. They are encouraged to explore beliefs that persons operating outside the values of Western culture might hold to be true. Finally, they are required to respond to situations using beliefs that are radically different from their own and to explore how such a change in personal orientation would alter other beliefs they hold. One result of value clarification should be movement toward a more open-minded approach to knowledge and events.

SUMMARY

Value clarification can contribute to the development of student skills in six areas of human interaction:

1. Communicating.
2. Empathizing.
3. Problem solving.
4. Assenting and dissenting.
5. Decision making.
6. Personal consistency.

When teachers plan and execute a systematic program of value clarification, students are likely to become more adept at using these skills. One approach to systematic value clarification will be presented in Chapter Two.

CHAPTER TWO

VALUE CLARIFICATION: AN APPROACH

Chapter One identified six reasons for planning and implementing value clarification activities. This chapter will present and explain one approach through which classroom teachers can make value clarification activities an integral element of instruction. More specifically, the intent of this chapter is to

1. Present definitions for two concepts—value clarification and the value sheet.
2. Describe four phases of value clarification in terms of the behavior of students during each phase.
3. Identify and provide examples of four modes of questioning that the teacher can use to facilitate value clarification.

When the ideas and concepts in this chapter have been mastered, a teacher should be able to select and use value clarification activities that are consistent with his instructional goals.

DEFINING VALUE CLARIFICATION AND THE VALUE SHEET

The terms "value clarification" and "value sheet," as used here, refer to distinct but interrelated concepts. *Value clarification* refers to verbal statements by students that can be used as a basis for inferring that students are comprehending, conceptualizing, and personalizing knowledge about humanity, society, beliefs, and culture. The *value sheet* is a learning device that (1) is designed to encourage students to express, examine, and organize their values and feelings; and (2) is planned and used as part of ongoing inquiries in the classroom. Value clarification thus refers to the student behaviors desired, and value sheet refers to planned learning activities designed to evoke these student behaviors. To review:

- *Value clarification* refers to patterns of student verbal behavior. The occurrence of these patterns can be used as a basis for inferring that students are comprehending and valuing knowledge about man, about society, and about themselves.
- The *value sheet* is a planned instructional activity or exercise.
- It is designed to elicit value clarification statements from students. Furthermore, these activities and exercises are designed and used as one aspect of organized units of instruction.

Value clarification is the ultimate goal and value sheets are a *means* for obtaining this end.

FOUR PHASES OF VALUE CLARIFICATION

Value clarification can be divided into four phases: (1) the *comprehension* phase; (2) the *relational* phase; (3) the *valuation* phase; and (4) the *reflective* phase. Each of these phases will now be described.

Phase I The Comprehension Phase

Phase I stresses student comprehension of a learning resource relevant to a concept, idea, or theme that is being learned, used, or evaluated. This resource can take numerous forms—a reading, a picture, a table of statistical data, a cartoon, a poem, a graph. During this phase, students are encouraged to identify and remember substantive data found in the learning resource. They are also asked to demonstrate their understanding of the data and ideas found in the resource.

Five categories of student statements are associated with this phase of value clarification. These five categories are *topical, empirical, interpretive, defining,* and *clarifying* statements. Given a resource, the teacher should expect to hear students expressing

1. *Topical* statements: verbally identifying the theme, topic, unit, idea, concept, or issue that is the focus of inquiry.
2. *Empirical* statements: listing specific and verifiable data from memory, especially when answering questions of *who, where, what,* and *when* with regard to a learning resource.
3. *Interpretive* statements: stating notions, opinions, interpretations, impressions, views, conjectures, estimations, and conclusions.
4. *Defining* statements: stating the meaning of a word or a term they are using.
5. *Clarifying* statements: rewording, rephrasing, restating, or elaborating on statements previously made, or indicating the context within which others are to understand statements being expressed or about to be expressed.

Empirical and interpretive statements are used conjunctively (in combination) during this phase. Students cite relevant data in the form of empirical statements and share ideas about the meaning of data in the guise of interpretive statements. This configurational (that is, combined) use of these two categories enables students to develop and share an understanding of the situation that is to be the object of valuation in Phase III.

Defining and clarifying statements are used to complement the use of empirical and interpretive statements. As students share ideas and establish a pool of shared data, the careful definition of key words and concepts helps them to avoid semantic confusion. Clarifying statements enable students to communicate the context within which their ideas and claims to knowledge are to be understood. Thus, the pattern of student language use associated with the comprehension phase can often be described as the configurational use of empirical, interpretive, defining, and clarifying statements.

Topical statements are used to help students identify or remember the topic of discussion. Unless such identification and retention are accomplished, students may experience difficulty maintaining focus. In addition, failure to establish the topic of discussion during the comprehension phase can weaken the relational and reflective phases of value clarification.

The primary function of Phase I is the comprehension of data relevant to an object of valuation. This function may require two, three, four, or five categories of student statements. When students have achieved an understanding of the object of valuation, they are ready to initiate the relational phase of value clarification.

Phase II The Relational Phase

The relational phase stresses student understanding and interpretations of data in light of the concept or theme that is the focus of ongoing inquiry. During this phase students search for and establish connections between the data and ideas they have learned in Phase I and the topic or idea being studied. Once this has occurred, students proceed to clarify further the relationships identified.

The categories of student statement associated with the relational phase are *topical, empirical, interpretive, defining, clarifying,* and *criterial.* During this phase, the teacher expects to hear students expressing

1. *Topical* statements: identifying the focus of discussion in order to relate data, interpretations, and ideas learned or reviewed during Phase I to the topic of study by naming the theme, the concept, or the topic that they are studying.
2. *Empirical* statements: identifying data they believe they can make relevant to the topic of study.
3. *Interpretive* statements: reviewing ideas learned during Phase I that can be related to the topic of study and building connections between the two.
4. *Defining* statements: defining words critical to the establishment of relationships between data and the topic of study.
5. *Clarifying* statements: clarifying the meaning of their statements by rewording, rephrasing, and elaborating.
6. *Criterial* statements: identifying the grounds or bases they have used, are using, or intend to use in order to establish relationships between data (empirical statements) and the topic or between ideas (interpretive statements) and the topic.

Five of the six categories included in this phase were also used to describe Phase I. These categories function differently in this phase in two ways. First, empirical and interpretive statements are used here to establish relationships between what has been comprehended and the topic of study. Second, criterial statements have been added to the patterns of language used during this phase.

During the relational phase, students use empirical, interpretive, and topical statements configurationally. Students may cite the focus of inquiry by using topical statements. They identify and list, in the form of empirical statements, data they believe to be relevant to the focus of discussion. They express connections between empirical statements and topical statements by using interpretive statements. On other occasions, students may cite empirical data, state the concept that is at the focus of study, and then interpret the data in terms of this concept.

When students claim that a connection exists between the topic of study and factual data, they can be asked to identify the grounds or basis for claiming this relationship. In so doing, students add criterial statements as another component of the pattern of language being used. As needed, clarifying statements and defining statements are used by students in order to clearly express themselves and in order to make themselves understood by others.

Phase II serves two functions. First, and foremost, the relational phase enables the teacher to use value clarification activities as an integral part of conceptually designed units. By stressing the interrelationships that can be found among data, interpretations, and the topic of study, the teacher avoids the danger that value clarification will be perceived as an isolated activity, walled off from the disciplined study of subject matter. Second, the relational phase focuses the attention of students and prepares them for Phase III.

Phase III The Valuation Phase

During this phase students react to a number of things by expressing values and feelings. They may react to the object of valuation, whether it is a situation, policy, event, or some other object that is to be valued; they may react to the concept or topic at the focus of study; they may react to relationships they established in Phase II; or they may react to any combination of these possibilities.

The valuation phase is associated with five categories of student statements: *preferential, consequential, criterial, imperative,* and *emotive.* During the valuation phase, the teacher anticipates hearing students expressing

1. *Preferential* statements: rating or ranking objects, events, situations, alternatives, concepts, consequences, and people, using such comparative words and phrases as good, better, best; bad, worse, worst; right, wrong; correct, incorrect; and adequate, most adequate, least adequate.
2. *Consequential* statements: suggesting known, expected, or anticipated results or effects of events, decisions, situations, policies, relationships, or actions.
3. *Criterial* statements: identifying the norms, assumptions, grounds, or bases by which they assign value ratings or make decisions about situations, relationships, policies, behaviors, or consequences.
4. *Imperative* statements: stating what ought or ought not to be done, what must or must not be done, what should or should not be true, what decisions have been made, what actions a person or group has decided to pursue or what possible alternatives to consider.
5. *Emotive* statements: conveying and revealing personal feelings, such as worry, fear, joy, love, happiness, contentment, excitement, or hate.

The valuing phase helps students learn to hold preferences, express emotions, and support policies in light of human consequences and criteria, and to hold preferences, express emotions, and make decisions while respecting the rights of others to the same privileges. Although student use of any one of these five statement categories is adequate for inferring that some valuation is occurring, value clarification is more reasonably inferred when students use a number of these categories configurationally.

When students suggest policies that ought to be adopted (imperative statements) and consider the benefits and costs of these policies to mankind (consequential statements), they use imperative and consequential statements configurationally. If students express personal feelings (emotive statements) and determine whether it would be good (or bad) for others to feel as they do (preferential statements), they use emotive and preferential statements configurationally.

It is not unusual for students to state positions involving three or more categories. If students identify policy alternatives (imperative statements), select the policy they believe is best (preferential statements), and state a basis for preferring this selection (criterial statements), they use three categories of the valuation phase configurationally. When students state feelings (emotive statements), determine the effects of these feelings with respect to the rights of others (consequential statements), differentiate between desirable and undesirable feelings (preferential statements), identify the basis for each preference (criterial statements), and generate consistent ideals (imperative statements), they employ all five categories configurationally. The extent to which students use these five categories as particular categories and as parts of a configurated language pattern influences the reflective phase of value clarification.

Phase IV The Reflective Phase

Phase IV of value clarification is designed to encourage students to reflect on the values and feelings they have experienced and revealed publicly in response to particular aspects of earlier phases. The reflective phase enables students to value the preferences and emotions experienced and objectified in response to a number of particular value-sheet episodes related to the same concept. Whereas Phases I, II, and III have the form of personal and conceptual value clarification, the reflective phase, by providing the opportunity for more reflective thought and insight, has the more substantial goal of making students aware of how they know, think, value, and feel.

Phase IV, then, is feasible only after a number of activities (value sheet episodes) relevant to the same conceptual focus have been made the object of learning, inquiry, analysis, and valuing. By creating a series of situations or resources through which students publicly state their beliefs and disbeliefs over a period of time, this phase enables students to examine and, if they wish, to reorganize their belief systems. This phase provides the opportunity for students to examine the consistency and likely consequences of their valuation behaviors. Because several value sheets related to the same concept are necessary in order to make Phase IV possible, this series of value clarification activities can aptly be referred to as a *valuing strategy.*

To illustrate the reflective phase of value clarification, suppose that students have studied a minimum of three value sheets relevant to the concept of separation of powers. Suppose further that they have comprehended each of the value sheets (Phase I), have established relationships between each value sheet situation or resource and the focusing concept (Phase II), and have expressed personal reactions in the form of preferential, consequential, criterial, imperative, and emotive statements (Phase III). At this point, students can reflect on their performance and can generate data, information, and ideas about their own behavior. In order to secure student reflection, the teacher helps his students to engage in four behaviors. The reflective phase of value clarification requires that students

1. Collect information about how they comprehended and assigned meaning to the data and concept they studied.
2. Collect and interpret information about how they framed, determined, and used relationships within the context of the concept and resource being studied.
3. Collect and interpret information about how they made decisions, identified and used norms, considered consequences, conveyed preferences, and expressed feelings.
4. Assign values to how they acquired knowledge, thought, behaved, organized preferences, and shared feelings, using such criteria as personal consistency, social consequences, and feasibility.

When students have met these standards they have engaged in and experienced all four phases of value clarification.

The value clarification theory presented here consists of four distinct yet interrelated phases. These are referred to as the comprehension, relational, valuation, and reflective phases. Phases I through III can be analyzed and described in terms of discrete categories of student behaviors that can be used configurationally to help students evolve understandings and achieve the expression of their values. The categories for each phase are reviewed in Figure 1. The fourth phase focuses attention on

CATEGORIES OF STUDENT STATEMENTS	PHASE I	II	III	IV
Topical	●	●		
Empirical	●	●		●
Interpretive	●	●		●
Defining	●	●		●
Clarifying	●	●		
Preferential			●	●
Consequential			●	●
Criterial		●	●	●
Imperative			●	●
Emotive			●	●

Figure 1 Categories of student statements associated with the four phases of value clarification.

student procedures and uses data germane to this task to help students analyze and value their belief system. The first three phases can be evoked from students through value sheets. When a number of value clarification episodes using value sheets relevant to a common theme have been implemented, then Phase IV is feasible. When this occurs, the four phases combined are referred to as a *value clarification strategy.*

VISUALIZING THE PHASES OF VALUE CLARIFICATION

As he plans and teaches for value clarification, the teacher observes, actively solicits, and reinforces student verbal statements relevant to the four phases of value clarification identified and discussed above. Of the four phases, Phases I, II, and III lend themselves to schematic presentation. The three diagrams presented in this section are designed to help the teacher visualize what is occurring and to better understand his instructional role during value analysis and clarification.

Phase I The Comprehension Phase

This phase is designed to get students to identify, list, and share information and knowledge about a situation or event that is to be the object of valuation. It helps students review the meaning of the concept being studied. Teacher questions during this phase help students to *comprehend* the resource being used and to review the meaning of key words and of the concept being studied. The teacher expects to hear students responding with *topical, empirical, interpretive, defining,* and *clarifying* statements. This phase is depicted schematically in Figure 2.

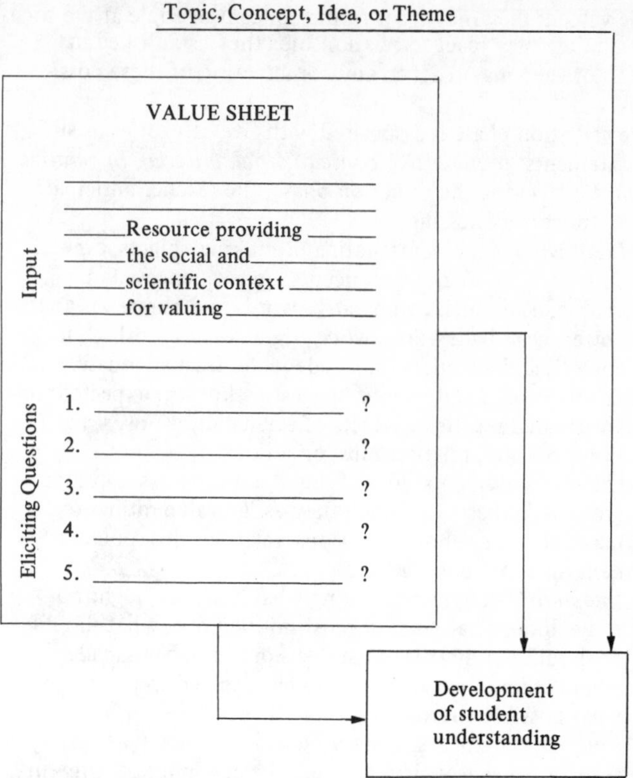

Figure 2 The comprehension phase.

Phase II The Relational Phase

This phase is designed to help students isolate data and associate it with the concept, topic, or idea being studied. It serves to help students connect the data in a learning resource to the focusing concept. It also serves to identify relationships between the resource material and the concept being explored. By raising questions, the teacher hopes to help his student generate, express, and elaborate connections and relationships. Student statements will take the form of *topical, empirical, interpretive, defining, clarifying,* and *criterial* categories of verbal behavior. This phase is depicted in Figure 3.

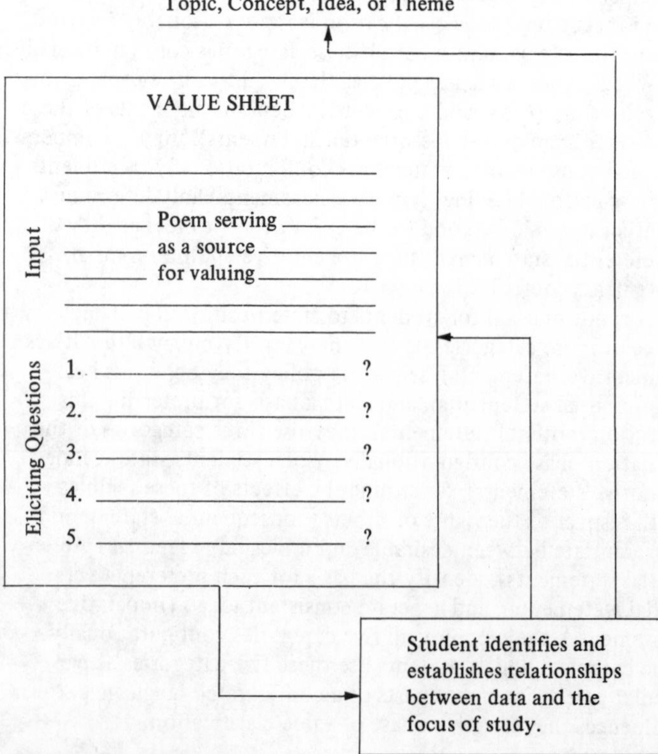

Figure 3 The relational phase.

Phase III The Valuation Phase
This phase is designed to get students to express their preferences and feelings toward such objects of valuation as data, situations, relationships, and decisions. During this phase, students consider and publicly state consequences, norms and grounds, alternatives, and decisions. During this phase, the teacher uses questions to help students objectify their values and feelings. The teacher expects to hear his students expressing *preferential, consequential, criterial, imperative,* and *emotive* statements in response to his questions. This phase is depicted schematically in Figure 4.

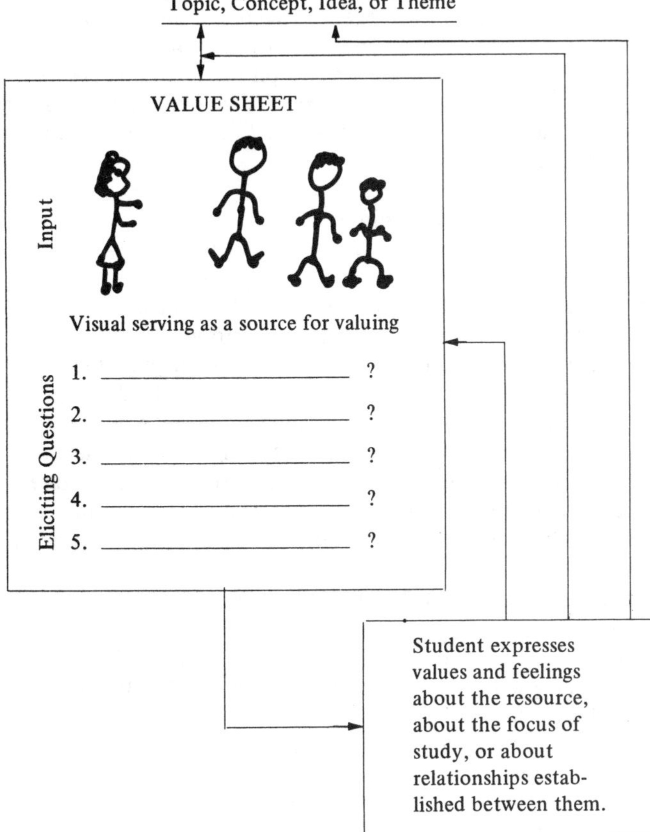

Figure 4 The valuation phase.

FOUR INTERROGATIVE MODES RELEVANT TO VALUE CLARIFICATION

Besides visualizing the first three phases of value clarification, the previous section pointed out the role of teacher questions in each phase. It was suggested that questions help the teacher elicit different phases of value clarification from his students. The classroom teacher can use questions in two ways: to plan and develop discussions that are appropriate for each of the phases so that his students can organize the data and their thoughts around the resource being used and the concept being studied, and to respond spontaneously and flexibly to student behaviors that occur during the course of guided inquiry. Because different kinds of questions are used to solicit different kinds of student responses, the teacher needs to have several modes of questioning or interrogative behavior at his disposal (Figure 5).

One effect of using different interrogative modes is that

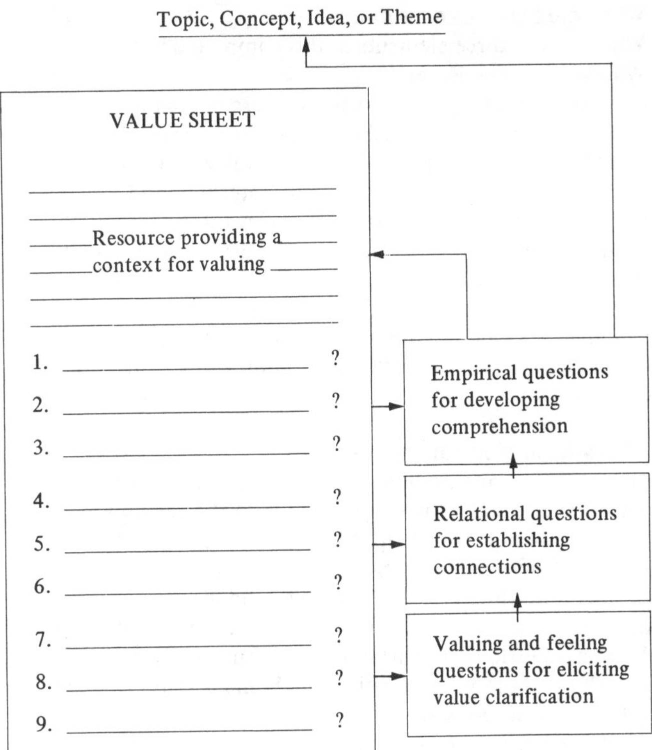

Figure 5 Relation of interrogative modes to value sheets and value clarification.

students and teacher are encouraged to move between the various phases of value clarification. A second effect is that it encourages the interphasic use of student language patterns. The advantage of employing these questions in this manner is that students feel freer to express their ideas, to share their values and feelings, and to refer to pertinent data with spontaneity. Without this degree of openness and flexibility, students are unlikely to feel secure or to perceive the interplay of knowing, thinking, and valuing as complementary elements useful for examining and clarifying social and personal values, beliefs, and preferences. The teacher who wishes to help students respond during value clarification activities will find four modes of questioning useful and applicable. These modes of interrogative behavior enable the teacher to focus and guide student attention during class discussion and assist him in becoming interphasic. They are (1) the *empirical* mode, (2) the *relational* mode, (3) the *valuing* mode, and (4) the *feeling* mode.

The Empirical Mode of Questioning

Empirical questions are employed when the teacher wishes to elicit statements of fact from students and to help them establish a pool of related data about a situation that is to be the object of valuation and value clarification. Some common examples of empirical questions are:

- What did you observe?
- What did you hear?
- What did the speaker say?
- What does your book say?
- In what year was this gadget invented?
- Who first discovered this element?

- When did Salk make his discovery?
- What are the three elements in this compound?
- Who wrote "The Raven"?

The teacher can use questions such as these in conjunction with a wide variety of learning resources and activities in order to help students identify and assemble data relevant to the situation they are expected to comprehend, interpret, and assign value to. Although often considered irrelevant, inappropriate, or unimportant in value clarification activities, this mode of questioning (and in particular, student responses to these questions) can play a vital role by assuring the teacher that statements made by students are based upon accurate information rather than baseless, inaccurate, or ill-founded personal opinions and notions.

The Relational Mode of Questioning

Relational questions are used when the teacher wants students to identify data and knowledge germane to the concept being studied. These questions help students connect the data and the resource material with the concept or topic being studied. Relational questions are also used when the teacher wants students to compare alternative ideas, policies, or ways of behaving. Relational questions are particularly relevant to the relational phase (Phase II) of value clarification. Some common examples of relational questions are:

- How is what you read related to our topic of study?
- In what ways are these ideas related?
- In what way is this information pertinent to our concept?
- What results of the experiment are most germane to the unit we are now studying?
- How would you compare the group's decision with your own decision?
- Are these two theories related to one another?
- How do the consequences of the third policy differ from those we listed for the first two policies?

The teacher can use questions similar to these in order to help students explore the relationships between different elements found in a situation or resource to be valued. Relational questions are used to generate student statements about the connections between and among different kinds of statements that have been expressed during class or small group discussion. If a teacher has planned, developed, and employed a value sheet in the classroom, and if a teacher expects students to consider their preferences in relation to the concept being studied by the class, he or she will make an effort to help students comprehend and understand the relationship between the value sheet and the concept being studied. Relational questions assist the teacher in guiding students to this end.

The Valuing Mode of Questioning

Valuing questions are employed when the teacher wishes to get students to publicly state and affirm value ratings they have assigned. These questions focus the attention of students on certain aspects of the situation they are asked to rate and guarantee that students affirm the values they assign. One might perceive value questions as aids to the teacher in eliciting assigned value ratings and preferences with regard to situations, resources, and actions. Common examples of valuing questions are:

- Is it good or bad for mankind that we continue to use scientific knowledge this way?
- Which of the consequences listed do you find most desirable?
- If all people felt as you feel, would this be good? For whom?
- Which of these policies would be the best one for us to follow?
- Is it wrong for scientists to pursue research in this area?
- Of the alternatives listed, which would be most harmful to mankind?
- Is it right for people to engage in activities such as these?

Valuing questions are used by the teacher to encourage students to determine, objectify, and publicly affirm their preferences. Valuing questions can be used to help students examine and reassess their value ratings with regard to such categories of statements as facts, relationships, consequences, interpretations, policies, and decisions. Because a major purpose of value clarification activities is to have students examine, explore, and consider their values, the teacher must incorporate this mode of questioning into the inquiry.

The Feeling Mode of Questioning

Feeling questions are utilized when the teacher wishes to elicit emotive statements from students. These questions provide the teacher with a mode of behavior he can use to make emotions an acceptable dimension of study in his classroom. When the teacher succeeds in eliciting emotive statements through the use of feeling questions, he provides his students with the opportunity to examine, reveal, and study human emotions related to life in society with others. By using the feeling mode of questioning, the teacher also helps other members of the class to comprehend better the choices and actions of their classmates during value clarification episodes. Some common examples of feeling questions are:

- How do you feel about the decision we have just made as a group?
- When you consider the facts, what are your feelings?
- Empathizing with the man in this story, how do you feel about his situation?
- When you first realized the nature of this relationship, what were your feelings?
- If this policy were to become law, how would you feel?

Because feelings are essential to human beings and because the feelings of participants during an inquiry are quite likely to influence their behavior, the recognition and legitimization of student feelings are not to be avoided or ignored. Feeling questions enable the teacher to objectify student feelings and to open these dimensions of student behavior to rational inquiry.

Teachers who wish to plan and use value clarification activities in their classrooms will find these four modes of interrogative teacher behavior relevant to their purpose and needs. The descriptions presented above are summarized and extended in Table 1.

SUMMARY

Value clarification may be defined as patterns of language that students use in order to convey their values to others. A verbal approach to value clarification provides classroom teachers with a frame of reference by which they can plan for and use value clarification activities systematically. In subsequent chapters, six types of value sheets that can be used to elicit value clarification language patterns from students will be identified and explained.

Table 1 Examples of the Four Interrogative Modes

EMPIRICAL	RELATIONAL	VALUING	FEELING
What did you see? What did you hear? What did you read? What did you observe? What did you experience? What do you remember? What happened?	How does what you saw relate to the topic? Explain your answer. How does what you heard relate to the topic? On what grounds? How does what you read relate to the topic? How does what you observed relate to the topic? On what basis? When you identified anxiety as a good consequence, how were you relating it to our topic?	Is the relationship you see good or bad for mankind? Explain. Is the event you experienced good or bad for mankind? Elaborate. Are the consequences of the relationship you established between facts and topic good or bad for mankind? Provide some illustrations. Would it be good or bad for mankind if we agreed with the feeling you just expressed?	How do you feel about what you saw? Heard? Read? Experienced? Remember? How do you feel about the relations we have established? How do you feel about the effort to base values on the concepts of human utility? If you found yourself in the situation we have described, what would be your most immediate feelings?

CHAPTER THREE

THE STANDARD FORMAT OF THE VALUE SHEET

One way of securing student value clarification is to plan and use value sheets. One format in which value sheets may be written is the *standard format* of the value sheet.

The classroom teacher will find that the standard format possesses a number of advantages. It can be designed and developed quickly and relatively easily for use with an ongoing instructional unit. It allows the teacher to incorporate two or three value sheets within the same instructional period, as it usually requires only fifteen to twenty minutes. The standard format also allows the teacher to present a wide variety of resources relevant to the same focus of study without giving students "the same old thing." The standard value sheet, like all the value clarification activities presented in this book, can be used to initiate a unit, can be incorporated within a sequence of activities, or can be used to culminate a unit of instruction.

The standard format is also useful for introducing systematic value clarification activities to students. It allows students to explore their values and feelings in a relatively nonthreatening environment and to gain familiarity and security in dealing with personal values and feelings as aspects of learning and knowing. As students feel more secure and comfortable in the examination and expression of personal preferences and emotions, the teacher can proceed to use other formats of the value sheet with some assurance that the students have developed readiness skills and attitudes.

The standard format contains two components: a learning resource providing the social or scientific context, and a set of questions relevant to the first three phases of value clarification.

The resource may be provided through any one of a variety of media available to the teacher and is selected in terms of its relevance to what students are studying at any particular time. Among the media that can be adapted and used to provide a social and scientific context for valuing are

cartoons	movies
poems	primary readings
magazine articles	selections from novels
cassettes	maps
filmstrips	selections from plays
graphs or charts	experiments
pictures	newspaper articles
field trips	television shows
personal letters	speeches
paintings	records

As the list suggests, teachers can vary the instructional media used for the standard format of the value sheet in order to arouse and maintain student interest.

A set of questions is designed to elicit student statements congruent with the comprehension, relational, and valuation phases of value clarification. These questions are intended to help students comprehend the resource, to connect the resource to the focus of inquiry, and to stimulate students to make decisions based upon their personal values and feelings. When this format is used, students are frequently asked to write their responses to these questions before participating in group discussion. The set of questions that students respond to should contain two or three questions designed to help students comprehend the resource selected as the focus of the activity; two or three questions designed to enable students to consider possible relationships between the resources and the concept, topic, or theme being studied; and one or two questions designed to help students examine and express their personal values and feelings with regard to the resource and topic, theme, or concept being studied

After students have written individual responses to these questions, the stage is set for public sharing and examining of personal preferences and feelings.

SAMPLES

Nine value sheets are presented here as samples of the standard format of the value sheet. Readers may wish to consider how they might adapt and use those examples that would be most relevant to their instructional goals and that would be of greatest interest to their students.

1. To Speak or Not to Speak

TEACHER PREPARATION

1. **Decide whether you wish students to read the resource portion of this value sheet and to respond individually to the discussion starters.**
2. **Secure sufficient copies of the value sheet for each student.**
3. **Before distributing the value sheet, ask students to read the First Amendment to the Constitution and ask them what this privilege means to them as individuals.**
4. **Adjust the discussion starters so that this value sheet becomes an integral element in the unit you are teaching.**

Resource Providing the Social and Scientific Context

Americans frequently talk about their legal rights under the Constitution and, more specifically, about the freedoms guaranteed to them by the Bill of Rights. However, it is often difficult to interpret the Constitution in order to use it as a guide in dealing with real-life situations. Suppose that as a citizen you knew that the following event had occurred in your community:

Bopper, a college student, received national attention after he organized a highly controversial meeting. At this meeting, Bopper called the President of the United States a criminal pervert. He referred to soldiers as legalized murders and to boy scout troops as the schools in which soldiers are trained to be deadly agents. He insulted the mayor of the town by referring to him with profane expressions. He urged those oppressed by the American system to get guns and to fight to secure their rights.

Bopper's speech made many of the people who attended the meeting quite angry. When police officers assigned to the meeting believed that Bopper might be in the process of creating a violent and explosive situation, they ordered Bopper to stop speaking. Bopper refused.

When Bopper attempted to resume his speech, police officers arrested and jailed him. The charge was disorderly conduct. Bopper was tried and convicted and served thirty days in jail.

After his release, Bopper argued that he had been denied his constitutional right to practice free speech. Those who believed that his arrest was proper and his punishment just argued that Bopper was not using but abusing free speech.

Discussion Starters

1. What did Bopper do in order to antagonize his audience?
2. Why do you believe Bopper behaved as he did?
3. Why did the police arrest Bopper?
4. In your opinion, to what degree, if any, was Bopper guilty of disorderly conduct?
5. Should the police have arrested Bopper? Justify your response.
6. Under what circumstances, if any, should Bopper's freedom of speech be limited?
7. Should people who don't believe in the American way of life or system of government be given the same freedom as those who do? Explain your response.

2. Little Garden Gates

TEACHER PREPARATION

1. **Decide whether you want each student to read the poem for himself or whether you want it to be read interpretatively to the class.**
2. **Develop questions likely to elicit each of the first three phases of value clarification.**

Resource Providing the Social and Scientific Context

Little garden gates,
Up and down the street,
Protecting dainty flowers
From little children's feet

The little garden gate
Might swing open at your will,
Open up a whole new world
Of wild street daffodils

But the little garden gate
May be forever closed
For fear of cold winds blowing
Leaving frostbite on the nose

Your little garden gate
Is entirely at your command
You can open up a world of truth
Or hibernate within.

(The authors appreciate the permission of Sharon Casteel to use this poem.)

Discussion Starters

1. To what does the phrase "garden gate," as used in the poem, refer?
2. The person who wrote the poem prefers wild flowers to domestic flowers. How do they differ in the poet's mind? How do they differ in your mind?
3. Does every person have a garden gate that he can open, close, and lock?
4. Suppose a person has new and original ideas. What kinds of frostbite does he risk for his nose?
5. What dangers does a person risk when he opens himself up to the world? What advantages does he obtain for running these kinds of risks?
6. Should a person believe that his garden gate is entirely at his command? Explain your answer.

3. The Sands of Ignorance

TEACHER PREPARATION

1. **Secure copies of the cartoon for each student, or convert the cartoon to an overhead transparency.**
2. **Prepare a list of discussion starters.**

Resource Providing the Social and Scientific Context

Discussion Starters

1. List six objects you see in the cartoon.
2. What subjects in school are associated with these objects?
3. What is the boy doing?
4. What does the title "The Sands of Ignorance" mean to you? What would be a more appropriate title for this cartoon?
5. What does this cartoon say about what one learns in school? Outside school?
6. What does this say about the kinds of information man has available to him for his use? The amount of information?
7. In what ways can increased information confuse a person? Make him more ignorant?
8. Should all "discovered knowledge" be made available to everyone? Why?
9. In what ways might an ignorant person be more secure than an informed person? Explain.
10. If ignorance is bliss, what is happiness?

4. Four Citizens of Integrity

TEACHER PREPARATION

1. **Secure sufficient copies of the value sheet for each student.**
2. **Consider making an overhead transparency of the diagram to use during class discussion.**
3. **Modify the discussion starters to preserve the integrity of the unit you are teaching.**

Resource Providing the Social and Scientific Context

For purposes of this value clarification activity, you are to consider the beliefs that four persons told about law, about order, and about law and order. The beliefs of the four persons may be diagramed as follows:

Citizen 2, Mr. Jones

"I believe that order and stability must be maintained at all costs. A man must feel secure in his home and safe to walk the streets. Those who would sacrifice order in order to maximize freedom are quite likely to make freedom meaningless. Innocent persons should not be punished; nevertheless, it is essential that all persons guilty of acts that threaten order and stability be given their just punishment."

Each citizen discusses his position briefly:

Citizen 1, Mr. Kurt

"I believe in law. Citizens should always be protected from unreasonable search and police interrogation. Those who seek order are most likely to be those who will risk the loss of man's basic freedoms. To the extent that the search for social order risks the freedom of individuals, those who believe in order are hostile to the basic rights of citizens. It is far better that criminals go unpunished than that a single innocent person be punished."

Citizen 3, Mrs. Lesseps

"Both social stability and the protection of the citizen through law are very important. However, when a decision must be made between the two, law should be protected at the expense of order."

Citizen 4, Mrs. O'Reilly

"Both social stability and the protection of the citizen by due process of law are very important. Nevertheless, in situations where a decision must be made in which either social stability or law is to be compromised, social stability must be protected at the expense of law."

Four Citizens of Integrity

Discussion Starters

1. How does Mr. Kurt's position differ from Mr. Jones's position with regard to law and order?
2. How does Mr. Kurt's position differ from that of Mrs. Lesseps?
3. How does Mrs. Lesseps's position differ from that of Mr. Jones?
4. How does Mrs. Lesseps's position differ from that of Mrs. O'Reilly?
5. Which of these positions most closely matches your own beliefs?
6. Which of the following makes you feel the best?
   a. Being secure.
   b. Being free.
   c. Protecting the rights of others.
7. Will citizens who possess integrity always make wise and good decisions? Explain your answer.

5. A Bar Tab

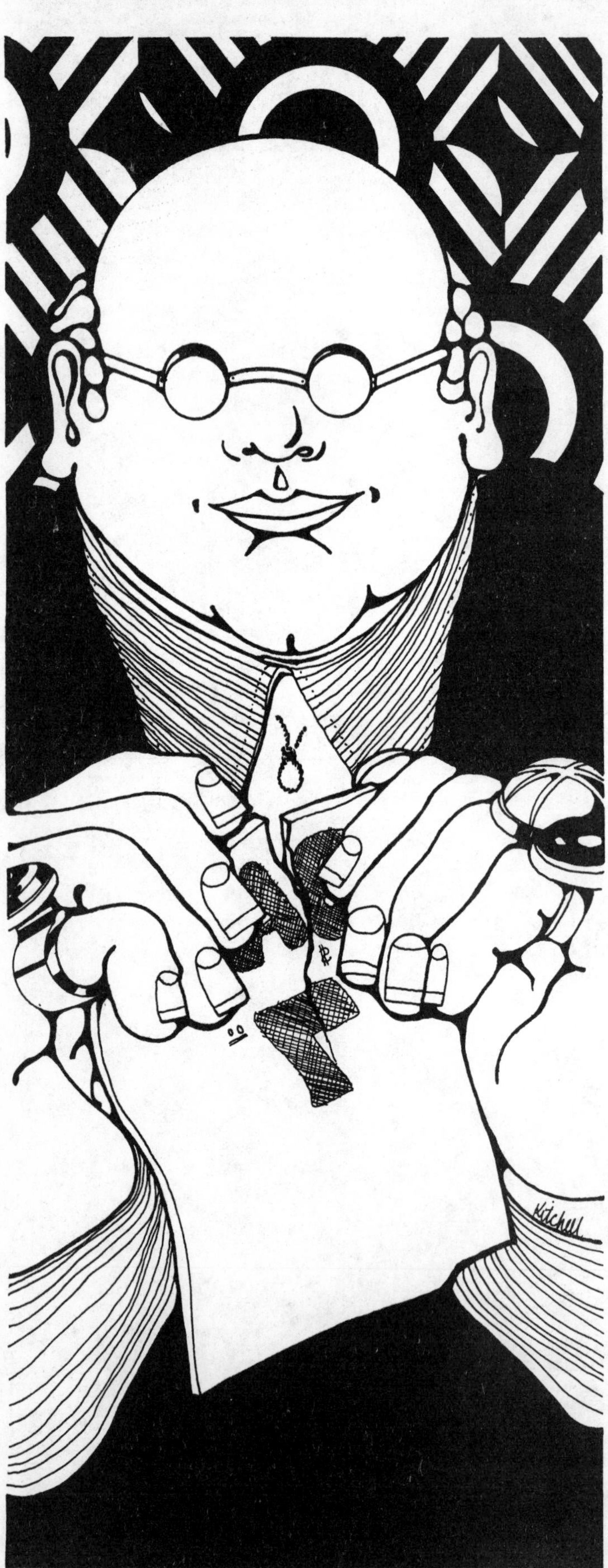

TEACHER PREPARATION

1. **Prior to using this value sheet, help students to develop definitions for the word "tolerance."**
2. **Decide whether you wish to assign students to role-play the situation as it is presented in the social and scientific context.**

Resource Providing the Social and Scientific Context

Yesterday John Watson was sentenced to five years in prison. Watson, an employee of a local convenience store, was found guilty of having stolen $7.00 from the cash register.

This evening a group of civic-minded citizens are eating dinner together in a private dining room of the local country club. Among those present at dinner is Judge Harkness, the Judge who sentenced Watson.

During the course of polite conversation, the Watson trial is mentioned. One of the diners compliments Harkness for his courage in "using the letter of the law to protect the entire community of Milltown."

A second speaker, not to be outdone, complimented Harkness for his wise and humane act. He proceeded to praise Harkness for "keeping young blacks in line thus protecting a satisfied black community from any illusion that a dissatisfied minority could bend the law in order to change their circumstances."

A slightly tipsy diner announced, with some difficulty, "You have shaped another future leader of our country and have thus helped to shape the destiny of America."

Caught up in the spirit of the occasion, the president of a local industry arose and announced that he would offer Watson a job upon his release from prison. "I want to show the world just how tolerant, concerned, and humane the citizens of Milltown are," he explained. For this announcement, he received a standing ovation from his fellow diners.

The conversation passed on to other topics and John Watson was quickly forgotten. Two hours later, as diners were preparing to leave, the manager of the country club appeared at the doorway.

The manager said, "Forgive me for disturbing you gentlemen, but we still have a bar check for $7.00 that has not been paid."

Before the manager could continue, one of those in the party said, "Forget it Harry. What's $7.00?" In response to this, those in the dining party laughed and applauded. As for the manager, he smiled his agreement and left.

Discussion Starters

1. Who is John Watson?
2. Given this reading, what does it mean to enforce the *letter* and ignore the *spirit* of the law?
3. Suppose that this reading is an example of what it means to be tolerant. In what sense could it be argued that tolerance is bad?
4. What should happen to John Watson? To Judge Harkness? To the diners?

6. The Strike Out

TEACHER PREPARATION

1. **Decide whether different parts of the class should react to the resource from labor's point of view, management's point of view, and the union's point of view.**
2. **Decide whether the resource is to be part of a role-playing activity, with students playing such roles as judge, businessman, "robber baron," labor leader, scab, union leader, nonunion worker, and so forth.**
3. **Decide whether the names of the brotherhood and the railroad are to be changed to fit the names of a union-management dispute you are currently studying.**
4. **Review the definitions of the following terms:**
   conspiracy
   brotherhood
   restrained
   injunction
   contempt of court
5. **Secure copies of the resource for those students who will need them.**
6. **Develop a list of discussion starters.**

Resource Providing the Social and Scientific Context

Western Central Railroad v. W.C.R.R. Brotherhood. The combination of laborers into an association that refuses to work except under conditions fixed by itself is an act of criminal conspiracy. Such a combination conspires to injure trade and commerce and places the public welfare in jeopardy.

A combination of laborers who are organized and who take action to raise their wages and improve their conditions can be considered in either of two ways: as a combination that will benefit its members, or as one that will injure those who did not join the combination. The law condemns both.

The facts of the instant case indicate that the Western Central Railroad Brotherhood, one such combination of laborers, has conspired to commit acts injurious to both trade and commerce. By walking out of their place of employment, by refusing to work, and by demanding higher salaries and better working conditions, the Brotherhood has committed criminal conspiracy.

The Brotherhood must be restrained from continuing such criminal actions; and so, the court grants the injunctive relief requested by the owner of the Western Central Railroad so that such criminal behavior can end and further injury can be prevented.

ORDERED, that the Western Central Railroad immediately cease and desist from the aforementioned criminal activity.

Failure to comply with this order will subject any member of the W.C.R.R. Brotherhood shown to be implicated in said failure to the contempt power of this court.

Discussion Starters

1. What specific acts committed by the labor brotherhood were labeled as "acts of criminal conspiracy" by the judge?
2. How do you think the court defined "the public welfare"?
3. What is the relationship between a court injunction and contempt of court?
4. Suppose this court decision was handed down during the post-Civil War era in America. Would the decision support or reject the principles of laissez faire as promoted by such men as John D. Rockefeller and Andrew Carnegie? Explain.
5. What will be the consequences to the brotherhood workers if they obey the court order? Disobey the court order?
6. Since the court has forbidden the brotherhood to strike for better conditions, what possible steps are now open to the brotherhood to pursue these same goals?
7. Suppose a group of young Americans were to propose that America return to the days when the principles of laissez faire reigned supreme. How would you feel toward accepting these principles and advocating their adoption by all Americans? Explain.
8. Is it good that America has empowered her courts to issue injunctions? Good for whom?

7. A Simple Question

TEACHER PREPARATION

1. **Prior to assigning this exercise, help students to develop definitions for the word "progress" and for the phrase "cultural lag."**
2. **Secure an overhead transparency of the cartoon that provides the social and scientific context.**
3. **Secure a copy of the discussion starters for each student and ask them to develop individual responses to each question prior to initiating group discussion.**

Resource Providing the Social and Scientific Context

(The authors appreciate the permission of Bhawhesh C. Mathur to adapt this cartoon.)

Discussion Starters

1. Describe what you see in the cartoon.
2. How would you answer the question posed in the cartoon's caption?
3. Are the objects shown in the cartoon related to progress? Explain.
4. Are "backyards" a sign of "cultural lag"?
5. What ought to be included in a "backyard"?
6. What are some of the advantages of having a "backyard"?
7. How would you feel if your own "backyard" was that shown in the cartoon?

8. Rats

TEACHER PREPARATION

1. **Secure sufficient copies of the resource.**
2. **Decide whether you wish students to respond to the questions individually or in small groups.**
3. **Develop questions likely to help students relate this value sheet to the unit you are teaching when you use it.**

Resource Providing the Social and Scientific Context

Chicago, Illinois—in a very stirring and emotional speech, the President last night declared an urgent need for Congress to act on a bill that would provide $237 million for the control of rats and mice in major urban centers. Addressing a fund-raising dinner, attended by persons capable of paying $1,000 for the right to a seat at the table, the President said, "This bill is needed and it is needed now. Congress should waste no more time in deliberation. Every minute of Congressional inaction and delay increases the threat of major epidemics in our cities."

The President continued his appeal by saying, "Disease-spreading rodents continue to flourish with no systematic effort being made to control them. The numbers of wild field mice and rats are at an all-time high. Should these rodents begin to breed with the urban rats, we could well be on our way to a plague unequaled in human history."

To this last appeal, the crowd roared with laughter, apparently believing that the President was jesting. However, the President was antagonized and continued to argue his case by . . .

MORE–MORE–MORE

Discussion Starters

1. Where is the President speaking?
2. What do you know about the President's audience?
3. What bill does the President want passed?
4. In your opinion, should the bill be passed?
5. Suppose the bill is not passed. What effect will this have on those in the President's audience?
6. If the bill is not passed, who are some of the people who will suffer?
7. What were your first feelings when you read that those whom the President was addressing laughed at his arguments?
8. Given what occurred here, could this President serve as an effective leader of the American nation? Explain your answer.

VOTE
NO
ON RATS
1000
N.

9. Growing

TEACHER PREPARATION

1. **Secure a copy of the value sheet for each student.**
2. **After having students read the poem individually, read, or ask students to read, the poem interpretatively.**
3. **Consider the possibility of asking a committee of students to design a bulletin board stressing the four verses in the poem.**

Resource Providing the Social and Scientific Context

You ask all those questions
that never are answered
Of wonder and awe
About the world around you.
Little one, why don't you grow up?

You talk to others
telling them your feelings
you don't understand
that you keep these things to yourself
so others can't hurt you.
Little one, why don't you grow up?

You love the woods
and cry when something dies
Everything dies eventually
You're alive, that's all that matters.
Little one, why don't you grow up?

You're too sensitive
always giving to people
when you should grab all you can get
before someone takes it first.
Little one, why don't you grow up?

(This poem was written by Bob Wallace. The authors appreciate his permission to adapt and use his poem.)

Discussion Starters

1. What is the central theme of this poem?
2. How old is the "little one" referred to in the poem? Which lines in the poem led you to this conclusion?
3. List four things the "little one" in the poem would have to do in order to be grown up.
4. How old is a person when he is all "grown up"?
5. Different societies use different devices to inform young people that they are grown and mature. Many societies have formal initiation rites for this purpose. Is the process of growing up in America ritualized? In what ways?
6. Should society place restrictions on the young that it does not place on adults? Justify your response.
7. Suppose you were the "little one" in this poem. What would growing up mean to you? How should you react to the advice that you grow up?

PROTOCOLS

All the value sheets in this chapter contained the two components essential to the standard format of the value sheet. Each contained a learning resource that provided the social and scientific context for the activity, and each contained a set of questions designed to elicit student statements consistent with the comprehension, relational and valuation phases of value clarification. Teachers finding these sample activities applicable to their own classroom will want to rewrite some of the questions to fit their unique instructional situations.

To design and develop a value sheet in the standard format to meet his or her particular needs, the teacher should

1. Identify the topic, concept, or theme of the unit of instruction.
2. Decide what preparations are necessary in order to properly introduce this value sheet.
3. Select a resource that is relevant to the topic, concept, or theme being taught.
4. Adapt this resource to fit the particular needs of the unit. (In other words, abstract or rewrite pertinent sections from a novel, a short story, a speech, or a long poem.)
5. Prepare a set of questions to elicit from students statements identified with the comprehension, relational, and valuation phases of value clarification.
6. Secure enough copies or make arrangements for all students to read or examine carefully the learning resource providing the social and scientific context. (Make copies, use the overhead projector, or use other means to make certain that students have ample opportunity to study and refer to the instructional resource.)
7. Consider how to make a smooth transition from the value clarification activity to the next activity planned for the instructional unit.

By following these procedures, teachers can develop original value sheets in the *standard* format that are similar to those presented in this chapter.

CHAPTER FOUR

THE FORCED-CHOICE FORMAT OF THE VALUE SHEET

The forced-choice format of the value sheet allows students to examine and make decisions about problems that occur quite often in their daily lives. This format focuses on those situations in which students must make a choice from among a number of almost equally attractive or almost equally unattractive alternatives. In trying to deal with such a condition, the student is faced with the realization that he cannot have all the alternatives and that the acceptance of one option means the automatic exclusion of the unchosen alternatives. Should he be presented with five very attractive or good alternatives, he must decide which one is the best. If his choice must be from among five very *un*attractive alternatives, he must decide which is the least unattractive. In either case he must consider the consequences of his decision. The forced-choice format offers the students the opportunity to engage in activities that not only allow them to make decisions in forced-choice situations but also help them to examine how such decisions, once made, are explained.

The forced-choice format usually contains four elements: (1) a narrative of a contrived or real problematic situation, (2) a listing of a limited number of options or alternative choices from which students must select the best one, (3) a decision sheet students use to identify their choice and to explain their decision, and (4) a set of questions, either written for students to complete or prepared to serve as guidelines for the teacher, to elicit student statements consistent with the comprehension, relational, and valuation phases of value clarification.

The forced-choice format can be created to emphasize a particular theme, topic, or concept. It can include a number of alternatives that have already been studied. The situations may be hypothetical or may be tied to practical everyday events and happenings. It may have a historical or futuristic setting. It may be adapted from a resource already used or currently being used in the classroom. Problematic situations can be abstracted from plays, magazine and newspaper articles, historical accounts, case studies, and current-event situations to provide background against which to establish a forced-choice condition.

The list of alternatives for the forced-choice format, usually three to five, should be directly relevant to the problematic situation in which the student is placed. These options are not intended to be exhaustive. The number of options available to the student should not be an extensive listing and should not contain a neutral or easy way out. Ideally, options should be either all desirable or all undesirable. The student must realize that he has but one choice and that when he has made that choice he has rejected the remaining options.

The decision sheet is relatively easy to develop in this format. A sheet of paper with appropriate directions will suffice. Each student is required to record his choice from among the alternatives given and to state in writing how he made his selection. The decision sheet allows the student who has made his decision to act upon it (by writing it down) and to become aware of the fact that others will be examining his decision in light of the criterion he uses in making his decision. By stipulating his criterion, he is saying that, of all the possible criteria he could have used, he valued these the most. The decision sheet allows each student to put down specific ideas and thoughts that may escape him if he is required to remember his decision and criterion over a period of time. It also tends to prevent the student from rapidly switching from choice to choice, since he has publicly expressed his original choice.

The forced-choice format also includes a set of questions. These questions are designed to help the student understand the problematic situation and the alternative choices from which he was "forced" to choose. They enable the student to identify and examine the connection between the problematic situation and the topic, concept, or theme being studied. These questions also enable the student to examine his preferences, especially as they relate to the grounds he uses and the consequences he considers in making his choice. These questions should not only emphasize the possible consequences of his particular choice but also the consequences that could have been expected had he selected one or more of the other choices. One difference exists between this set of questions and the set contained as part of the standard value sheet. The questions prepared for the forced-choice format are designed to guide the thinking and the questioning pattern of the teacher and are not usually included with the value sheet activity as items to which students respond in writing. However, there are times when the inclusion of such questions at the end of the forced-choice format are appropriate.

SAMPLES

Six examples of the forced-choice format of the value sheet follow. Teachers may find it useful to assume the role of students and to respond to examples as they believe their students would respond.

10. Critic's Choice

TEACHER PREPARATION

1. **Secure sufficient copies of the value sheet for each student who will participate in the value clarification episode.**
2. **Place a glossary on the board to assist students with terms you believe they will find difficult.**
3. **Develop questions that will help students relate their experience with this value sheet to the unit that you are teaching.**
4. **Decide whether each student is to respond individually or whether students are to work in groups of four or five.**

Social and Scientific Context

Recently, television programing has been subjected to harsh criticism. Newspapers and news magazines have attacked the superficial way in which news is presented. Prominent members of the bar and of the American Civil Liberties Union have attacked national efforts to engage in news analysis, basing their criticism on the tendency of such analysis to shape rather than assess public opinion. Leading consumer advocates have published books exposing the fact that television programers are not sensitive to their social responsibilities. Congressional committees are considering a number of bills to regulate the television industry and to curb abuses. In effect, a general mood has developed in which television programing is believed to be an insult to the intelligence of the American people.

Neither the attacks nor the mood has gone unchallenged. Representatives of the television industry have pointed with pride to their in-depth coverage of significant events. Script writers and television personalities have defended their work as new art forms consistent with television as a medium of communication. Influential politicians have referred to freedom of the press as too vital a freedom to be limited by law. A number of newspaper commentators have questioned the motives of leading Congressmen who are proposing bills and have cautioned the reading public to avoid participating in a witch hunt.

When one analyzes the debate, five policies can be detected. Each policy, having both its supporters and its opponents, is the focus of conflict, of argument, and of rhetoric. Following is a presentation of each policy, with a brief summary of the arguments offered by its proponents.

Policy A — Successful television programing has been and should continue to be based on *audience appeal.* Supporters of this policy argue that each fall the major networks offer new programs to the viewing public. By Thanksgiving, the viewing public has decided which shows should be kept and which shows should be withdrawn. Furthermore, new shows are constantly redesigned to win the favor of the viewing public. To the degree that the viewing public owns television sets with channel selectors, they can serve as their own critics and vote by turning the knob. To oppose this policy one must be an elitist, opposed to the general will as the will of the people expresses itself democratically.

Policy B — Successful television programing is and should always be a matter of *free enterprise.* It is part of a business and the goal of business is to show a profit. Because television programers must operate as free enterprisers and sell their own shows to the public, they can always be assumed to be sensitive to the needs and interests of the viewing public. Any step taken to control programing for some abstract social good erodes the American spirit of free enterprise and attacks the commitment of Americans to the value of being self-reliant. The entire American system of government was founded on economic free enterprise in the hands of self-reliant men. To oppose this policy is to be socialistic and to attack the very foundations of American freedom.

Policy C — Successful television programing is and should continue to be *pluralistic* in content and style. The wide spectrum of shows and the diverse nature of special programs is based on the varied nature of the American viewing audience. It does offer, and must continue to offer, a broad selection of programs at different levels of quality and sophistication to match the entertainment and information needs of the American public as it is, not as some would wish it to be. To oppose this policy is to be unfortunately idealistic and to practice intellectual snobbery.

Policy D — Television is and should continue to be primarily an *educational* medium. Unfortunately, current programs tend to teach the wrong things—frequently with disastrous results. Thirty-minute situation comedies teach the public that the worst of problems can be solved to everyone's satisfaction in thirty minutes. Detective, western, and mystery shows teach violence and have offered instruction in such matters as planting bombs and hijacking airplanes. Violent scenes in Saturday morning children's programming have taught youngsters to fight. Americans are robbed of their sensitivity to hardship, to the inevitability of conflict, and to the harmful effects that often follow physical conflict. In addition, they are offered few opportunities to appreciate the ironies and tragedies of life. Therefore, strict controls should be exercised, assigning a fair share of prime time to serious plays, symphonic concerts, poetry readings, and similar programs. Such programing is likely to challenge Americans to grow intellectually and morally. To attack such a policy is to be anti-intellectual and antisocial.

Policy E — The purpose of television programing is to help Americans use *leisure time.* Television programing has been and should continue to be aimed at helping Americans relax. Americans live, work, and play in a highly complex society. They return to their homes from school, from office, and from factory to relax and relieve tensions that they cannot escape in the world outside the home. Serious entertainment is available in the theater and in the concert hall. Public issues can be examined and analyzed by attending public lectures and doing serious reading in libraries. To resist the use of television for purposes of helping Americans to relax requires that one ignore the complex nature of our society. To question the correctness of this policy is to deny the general public an opportunity to use leisure time in order to recreate itself. To attack this policy in favor of more serious programing is to be an egghead.

Critic's Choice

After studying these five policies you decide to write your Congressman. You intend to inform him as to your personal position in the debate. In order to outline your letter, you select the policy you believe is best and list what you believe to be three good reasons why your Congressman should believe as you do. A worksheet for this purpose is provided here.

WORKSHEET

The best policy to follow with regard to television programing is: ______

______

______

______

______

______

Good reasons for adopting this policy are:

1. ______

______

______

2. ______

______

______

3. ______

______

______

Critic's Choice

Discussion Starters

1. What reasons did different critics give for attacking television programing?
2. What were the names of the groups and agencies that attacked the television programers? What right did each have to make such criticisms?
3. Suppose your policy were used as the basis for federal legislation affecting *all* future television programs. How would each of the following groups in our society be affected by these program changes?
   a. Preschool children who spend all day at home.
   b. Retirees who remain at home most of the day.
   c. Housewives, especially those with young children.
   d. Students attending school during school hours.
   e. Teenagers after school and during the weekend.
4. In reference to question 3, which group would most benefit from the adoption of your policy? Explain. Which group would be most adversely affected by its adoption? Explain.
5. In what ways are freedom of the press related to our "right to know"?
6. There is an old adage that "no news is good news." Would restrictions on the freedom of television news coverage and reporting limit the amount of total news, good news, or bad news broadcast to television viewers? Explain.
7. When does news become "bad"?
8. Who should be responsible for making decisions about the programs shown on television? How do you justify their right to make such decisions?

11. A Small Search for Elusive Reasons

TEACHER PREPARATION

1. **Secure sufficient copies of the value sheet for each class member to have a copy.**
2. **Divide members of the class into discussion groups of four to seven members each, allowing students to select their own groups.**
3. **Provide instructions to the effect that each group is to make a decision and to find reasons that will justify the decision they make.**
4. **Explain that there are no right or wrong decisions; that any decision they make and can provide grounds for is most appropriate.**
5. **Although optional, secure one page of newsprint and one felt pen for each group to assist students in sharing their decisions and criteria with one another.**

Social and Scientific Context

A mongoloid child was born with a defective digestive tract that was sure to cause his death by starvation if not corrected. Correction involved a relatively simple operation. The child's mother refused to permit the operation because she felt she could not give adequate care or love to the defective infant and because she felt the mongoloid child's living would cause great harm to her three normal children. Faced with this refusal, the doctors recognized four possible courses of action:

1. They could ignore the mother and operate anyway.
2. They could consent to the mother's desire and allow the baby to starve to death.
3. They could inject an air bubble into the baby's bloodstream, killing him painlessly and quickly.
4. They could seek a court order to perform the operation as a legal right of the child.

Given only these four choices, the doctors should have:

____

____

____

Of the four choices, this is best because: ________________

____

____

____

____

____

____

____

____

Discussion Starters

1. Which groups agreed as to what was to be done? Which disagreed?
2. What grounds were offered for different decisions?
3. What grounds were offered for the same decision? How do you explain people making the same decision and giving different reasons?
4. Did different groups, by any chance, offer the same ground but recommend different policies? How could this occur?
5. Based on the way we have behaved, how do we believe that life should be defined and protected?

A Twentieth-Century Auction

12. A Twentieth-Century Auction

TEACHER PREPARATION

1. **Secure copies of the social and scientific context for each student. Read aloud or describe the situation presented in the background leading to the decision.**
2. **Decide whether the class is to be divided into small groups for this activity or whether only one small group is to be formed, with the rest of the class serving as audience and potential critics.**
3. **Secure copies of each of the five consequential analysis forms and the one final decision form for each student.**
4. **Prepare a list of discussion starters to follow the panel decision.**

Social and Scientific Context

For purposes of this exercise you are to assume that you live in a town of about 50,000 people. When those citizens who live within your county but outside the city limits are included, the total population of your county is about 80,000 persons. You are a concerned citizen, well known for your work in various civic projects, such as the annual United Fund Drive, the Biracial School Advisory Committee, and the annual county fair. Although you have never run for public office, you are respected as a well-informed citizen and a person of honesty, character, and good judgment.

The governing body of your county is made up of seven county commissioners. These seven persons are responsible for lands that belong to the county. Among such land holdings, the county owns three public parks, operates a bird sanctuary, and maintains a small natural wilderness. In addition, the county owns an eighty-acre tract of land immediately west of the city limits. This land, formerly a prosperous dairy farm, is undeveloped, and the county does not have adequate funds to develop it.

When the title to this eighty acres was obtained by the county, officials had hoped to secure state and federal funds to develop the land for civic purposes. Efforts to secure these funds have consistently failed. Realizing that future efforts offer no better prospects of success, the county commission voted to sell the land and use the revenue to improve the three parks already in operation. With this decision made, the land was described and offered for sale, and sealed bids were accepted. The county received five bids, with each bidder offering about $162,000 for the property.

Under normal circumstances, the land would be sold to the highest bidder. However, an investigative reporter has discovered that the highest bidder might have had access to information denied to the other four bidders. Law suits are intimated. The county commissioners fear that they will lose the confidence of citizens. As a result, the five bidders and the county commission arrive at an agreement: A panel of citizens should study the five bids and decide who is to get the land. They also agree that inasmuch as the five bids are almost equal, the panel should consider the general welfare of the community as the primary basis for making its decision. You are asked to serve as a member of this decision-making panel, and you accept.

According to the agreement developed by the five bidders and the county commissioners, there are some rules that your panel must follow:

1. Prior to making a decision, the panel is to determine how each bidder proposes to use the land, what the land will look like after it has been developed, and what the good and bad consequences of each bid would be. This will provide the county commission with a consequential analysis of alternative proposals and enable both bidders and citizens to know how the panel reasoned in order to make a decision.
2. After a consequential analysis has been developed for each bid, the panel is to select the bidder who is to be allowed to purchase the land and to identify the *single* most important reason for this choice.
3. Forms developed and agreed to by the bidders and the county commission are to be used for this purpose.

The forms necessary to complete your task as a member of the panel follow. Before beginning to use these forms, make sure that you understand the situation and your role.

CONSEQUENTIAL ANALYSIS FORM

Bidder A He represents a private corporation that specializes in the sale and distribution of fertilizers, pesticides, and herbicides in bulk quantities to farmers who wish to do their own work. However, the products sold by the corporation are normally spread by crop-dusting planes. Because of its location—near the center of a five-county commercial farming region—the land will become the focus of a regional business serving five counties of the state. Much of this land will thus be converted to an airfield with runways, hangars, docking facilities, and the like.

If Bidder A obtains the land, the following statements describe how the land will be used:

1. ______________________________

2. ______________________________

3. ______________________________

Beneficial results of selling the land to Bidder A include:

1. ______________________________

2. ______________________________

3. ______________________________

4. ______________________________

Undesirable results of selling the land to Bidder A include:

1. ______________________________

2. ______________________________

3. ______________________________

4. ______________________________

Bidder B He represents a company that has received a grant to explore the possibility of restoring dirigible air transportation. Members of the company have bought similar tracts elsewhere and are interested in this piece of land because it is central to a number of tourist attractions. These attractions are likely to lure persons to try dirigible travel and to become acquainted with this form of flying. The company plans to build an airfield, hangars, and a resort hotel.

If Bidder B obtains the land, the following statements describe how the land will be used:

1. ______________________________

2. ______________________________

3. ______________________________

Beneficial results of selling the land to Bidder B include:

1. ______________________________

2. ______________________________

3. ______________________________

4. ______________________________

Undesirable results of selling to Bidder B include:

1. ______________________________

2. ______________________________

3. ______________________________

4. ______________________________

A Twentieth-Century Auction

Bidder C He represents a group of private citizens that has just negotiated a contract with the armed forces to help keep its paratroopers physically ready and well trained in the art of parachuting. The land would house equipment for training the reservist paratrooper in the most recent developments in skydiving and parachuting techniques. Besides the warehouse for equipment storage, several runways and accessory buildings and materials will be built on the land.

If Bidder C obtains the land, the following statements describe how the land will be used:

1. ______________________________

2. ______________________________

3. ______________________________

Beneficial results of selling the land to Bidder C include:

1. ______________________________

2. ______________________________

3. ______________________________

4. ______________________________

Undesirable results of selling the land to Bidder C include:

1. ______________________________

2. ______________________________

3. ______________________________

4. ______________________________

Bidder D He is a private individual who wants to fulfill his lifelong ambition of owning his own small plane facility. He plans to sell, service, repair, and renovate privately owned aircraft. He believes the area is ideal for test flying the aircraft he works on and for demonstration flights of new equipment. The land will provide space for sales, runways, shops, hangars, and testing equipment. He anticipates that the facility will be kept busy due to a growing interest in flying.

If Bidder D obtains the land, the following statements describe how the land will be used:

1. ______________________________

2. ______________________________

3. ______________________________

Beneficial results of selling the land to Bidder D include:

1. ______________________________

2. ______________________________

3. ______________________________

4. ______________________________

Undesirable results of selling the land to Bidder D include:

1. ______________________________

2. ______________________________

3. ______________________________

4. ______________________________

A Twentieth-Century Auction

Bidder E He represents a nationally known glider club. His club wants the property because of its ideal location for gliding. If the club is successful in its bid, it plans to move its national headquarters to your city. Semiannual national glider competitions will be held at the airfield that is to be built. As its budget permits, the club will build runways, hangars, docking facilities, repair shops, office space, a cafeteria, and a motel. In addition, gliding instruction will be made available.

If Bidder E obtains the land, the following statements describe how the land will be used:

1. ______________________________

____

2. ______________________________

____

3. ______________________________

____

Beneficial results of selling the land to Bidder E include:

1. ______________________________

____

2. ______________________________

____

3. ______________________________

____

4. ______________________________

____

Undesirable results of selling the land to Bidder E include:

1. ______________________________

____

2. ______________________________

____

3. ______________________________

____

4. ______________________________

____

A Twentieth-Century Auction

FINAL DECISION FORM

The land is to be sold to Bidder ______ .

The *single most important reason* for selecting this bidder is: ______________________________

____

____

____

____

____

Signatures of members making this decision:

____

____

____

____

____

A Twentieth-Century Auction

Discussion Starters

1. Why did the county commission want to sell the eighty acres of land?
2. What reasons were given for the selection of the panel to decide the fate of the eighty acres?
3. How would you define the "general welfare of the community"?
4. Why do governments prefer sealed bids to a set price? To public auction?
5. In what ways was the "bad news" revealed by the reporter really good news? Explain.
6. Suppose your state had a law requiring governments to do public business "in the sunshine." In what ways would sealed bids be a violation of this law?
7. Is it always good to have government agencies do all of their public business "in the sunshine"? Explain. When might it be bad to conduct business this way?

13. A Question of Accountability

TEACHER PREPARATION

1. **Secure a copy of the paragraphs describing each car or vehicle for each student.**
2. **Secure a copy of the social and scientific context for each student to read, or read it aloud yourself, or describe the situation in which the student role-playing a highway patrolman is expected to make a decision.**
3. **Prepare a copy of the discussion starters for each student.**
4. **Determine whether you wish to divide students into small groups of four to seven in order to continue this activity. (In this value sheet, all students are to make an individual decision. This may be followed by small group interactions.)**

Social and Scientific Context

You are a policeman observing the flow of traffic across a narrow bridge during a sudden and blinding thunderstorm. Traffic has slowed to a snail's pace, and visibility is near zero. The narrow bridge spans a normally sluggish creek that has been transformed into a raging current by the cloudburst. As you watch, an automobile stalls, its engine drowned out. You leave your patrol car and begin to direct traffic until the stalled car can either be restarted or removed to the side of the road.

While this is occurring, another driver leaves his car and approaches you with a message. He claims to have heard a very important radio announcement. He tells you that flash floods and unexpected volumes of water have washed out two bridges upstream. The radio announcer has further stated that all bridges downstream are being closed to all traffic until the storm abates and the level of water in the stream subsides.

You radio headquarters and confirm that the news announcement is correct. Immediately, you commandeer the stalled car and use it to block the western approach to the bridge. This step accomplished, you drive your patrol car across the bridge and use it to block the eastern approach to the bridge. With the bridge effectively barricaded, you again radio headquarters to report that you have closed the road. At this time the dispatcher provides you with further information and directions:

- The department of transportation will set up barricades and warning lights as quickly as possible.
- At the rate the creek is currently rising, both the eastern and western lowlands through which the highway winds will be flooded within thirty to forty-five minutes.
- Weather forecasters predict continued precipitation for the next twenty-four to thirty-six hours.
- Under normal circumstances you are to permit no one to cross the bridge. You are authorized to permit *one vehicle* to cross the bridge in the event of an emergency, provided the driver of the vehicle is informed of the dangers and crosses at his own risk. There will be *no authorized* exceptions to this rule.
- All aircraft have been grounded by the Federal Aviation Agency.
- Should decisions and authorizations not provided for by these conditions become necessary, you are to use your best judgment with the full awareness that you are accountable for your actions.

Having received this information, you sign off and walk back across the bridge to set up flares in advance of the stalled car you have used to block the western approach to the bridge. (You also want to pass word down the line of blocked traffic that the drivers have only thirty minutes in which to avoid being trapped by rising water.) As you cross the bridge, the roar of the water seems to rub your spine like a cold finger, and you imagine that you can hear the bridge groaning in its effort to hold against elemental forces.

Suddenly, new sounds reach your ears, and in the distance, from the west, you can dimly perceive revolving lights, some blue and some red. Five emergency vehicles are headed for the bridge: a highway patrol car, a sheriff's car, an ambulance, a fire engine, and a postal vehicle carrying mail. Their arrival at your improvised barricade occurs almost simultaneously. Realizing that you are authorized to allow but one vehicle to cross the bridge, you decide to determine the purpose of each vehicle in order to isolate which, if any, of the vehicles you will allow to proceed across the bridge.

The Sheriff's Car A deputy sheriff is on his way to another bridge downstream, where no one has stopped traffic yet. Unless the deputy sheriff is allowed to proceed, an imminent collapse of the bridge may take innocent lives, for which you will be held accountable. This is the only available sheriff's car for this purpose.

The Highway Patrol Car This car is being driven by a captain of the highway patrol appointed to this mission by the governor. A leading contender for the presidential nomination of his party has been wounded in an attempted assassination. He has survived the attack but is in dire need of a rare type of blood; unless the blood being transported in the highway patrol car reaches him within the next two hours, his chances for living are minimal. Furthermore, the blood has been carefully packaged in a refrigerated container that works in conjunction with the air-conditioning system built into the highway patrol car. Any significant change in its temperature is likely to make the blood unusable. If you deny passage to the highway patrol captain, you may be responsible, and held accountable, for the unnecessary death of the presidential aspirant.

The Ambulance This vehicle is transporting two severely injured persons, a woman in her seventh month of pregnancy who is hemorrhaging and her twelve-month-old son. Both have serious internal injuries. To delay their treatment in intensive-care units at the hospital is to sentence the woman, her son, and her unborn baby to death. The driver and attendant refuse to risk any movement of the victims to another vehicle.

The Fire Engine This vehicle is rushing to help put out a fire that is raging through an apartment complex limited to the aged and infirm. The three-story structures involved house several hundred elderly persons, perhaps as many as a thousand. Lightning has struck a television antenna, causing a television set to explode and ignite the blaze. No one knows how many, if any, of the occupants are trapped or injured. Other fire engines are expected to follow. To deny passage to the fire truck is to risk being accountable for a major human tragedy.

The Postal Vehicle This vehicle is delivering mail on its assigned mail route. It is carrying an assortment of pension and social security checks as well as other types of mail. The highway is a United States highway and, as such, is legally a post road. To deny passage to this vehicle is to deny a postal truck the use of a post road.

MAIL
AMBULANCE
SHERIFF

A Question of Accountability

A Question of Accountability

Discussion Starters (A Student Response Guide)

1. The situation in which I am asked to make a decision can be summarized as:

2. Having made the best possible decision, my decision was:

3. When I think about the decision I have just made, the thing that worries me the most is:

4. The values on which I based my decision were:

5. The consequences to myself that I have risked are:

6. Using this decision as a basis, I wonder whether having power over who will live and who will die makes one feel powerful because:

14. The Prisoner Will Stand Up

TEACHER PREPARATION

1. **Secure sufficient copies of the value sheet for each student to have a copy.**
2. **Prior to having students make a choice, make sure they understand the context.**
3. **Decide whether you want to have students dramatize this event. If so, select a judge, a Miss Waldrop, and a jury.**
4. **Determine how you will integrate this value sheet into your unit of work.**

Social and Scientific Context

The time is 1877. The place is a courtroom in an American city. A trial is about to end.

The trial has been too short to suit the defendant, Miss Anne Waldrop, who has been charged with illegally voting during the last presidential election. The defendant had been prepared to bring in dozens of witnesses, women friends, and members of the local women's rights league. But the judge (Judge Dauber) announced that only those directly involved in the case would be allowed on the witness stand and that his court was not going to be a soapbox for every Jane, Ann, and Mary to use to support their cause. After a day and a half of testimony, the prisoner has been brought before Judge Dauber for sentencing. The following is an account of the proceedings of the closing minutes of the trial.

Judge Dauber: The court orders the prisoner to stand up and come before the bench to hear the decision of the jury. Before pronouncing the decision of the court, have you, Miss Waldrop, anything to say as to why this sentence should not be pronounced?

Miss Waldrop: Yes, I have, Your Honor. While there are many things I would like to say, I would like to emphasize only those that are most important, for in this court you have already trampled every vital principle and civil right of our government. The sentence that you are about to read is a court-ordered verdict of guilty. My rights, whether they be my natural rights, my political rights, my civil rights, or my judicial rights, have all been refused me and ignored by this court. I have been robbed of all my fundamental privileges and rights of citizenship in this, the land of the free. I have been degraded from the status of a citizen to that of a subject. Even worse, all of my sex will be, by Your Honor's decision, doomed to political and legalized subjugation under this so-called democratic government.

Judge Dauber: This court will not stand by and listen to the defendant restate the same arguments presented by the defendant's counsel earlier this morning. The court especially wants to remind the defendant that her arguments consumed nearly three hours of the court's time, ample opportunity to include any meaningful and useful arguments to support the defendant's case. Such repetition is not appropriate now.

Miss Waldrop: May it please Your Honor, I do not wish to argue the question. I am simply trying to state the reasons why this guilty sentence cannot and should not, in justice, be pronounced against me. By denying me my legitimate right as a citizen of this nation to vote for the administrators of the government, you have denied me my right of consent as one of the governed, my right of representation as one of the taxed, and my right to a trial by jury of my peers as an offender against law. But most of all, your denial of my citizen's right to vote is a denial of my sacred and natural rights of life, liberty, property, and . . .

Judge Dauber: The court will not and cannot allow the prisoner to go on!

Miss Waldrop: So! Your Honor persists in denying me my rights! Will you also deny me this one and single privilege of protest and speech against this single-handed attack upon my citizen's rights? Now you have taken away my rights and want to refuse me any privileges that I at least thought, maybe mistakenly, that I had some access to as a person living in this country. May it please the court to remember that since the day of my arrest last November, this is the very first time that either I or any person of my sex has been allowed a word of defense before judge or jury. I am dismayed that . . .

Judge Dauber [*Rapping the bench with his gavel*]: The court cannot allow this behavior! The prisoner must sit down immediately!

Miss Waldrop: My prosecutors, every one of them, from the third-ward drug store politician who entered the complaint, to the federal marshal, the commissioner, the district attorney, the district judge—even Your Honor on the bench—not one of them is my peer; but each and all are my political sovereigns. As if this were not bad enough, had Your Honor submitted my case to the jury, as was clearly your duty, I would still have had just cause to protest, for not one of those men was my peer. Each and every man, native or foreign born, white or black or red, rich or poor, educated or ignorant, sober or drunk, awake or asleep, informed or uninformed, healthy or ill, employed or unemployed, is my political and legal superior. That leaves me with only the one belief that, in a sense, I have no peers except for those of my own sex, and I can never be a peer among men regardless of their lot in life or mine. Even a commoner of England, tried before a jury of lords, would have far greater chance of receiving a fair trial and would have far less cause to complain and protest than I, a woman, tried before a jury of men. Even my astute counsel, Stephen O. Senger, who has argued my cause so ably and so energetically before this court and before Your Honor, is my political sovereign. No disfranchised person is entitled to sit upon a jury, and women are not entitled to the franchise. No one except a regularly admitted lawyer can practice in the courts, and with women prevented from being admitted to the bar, judge, jury, and counsel must all be members of the true sovereign class of America—men.

Judge Dauber: The court must order the prisoner to cease this disturbance. Miss Waldrop, you are running the risk of being charged with contempt. The prisoner has been tried according to the established procedures of law and justice in this land.

Miss Waldrop: Yes, you're right, Your Honor. I have been tried according to the established procedures of law and justice, but may I again remind the court, and Your Honor, that these procedures, the law, and the form of justice were all devised by men, interpreted by men, administered by men, in favor of men, and enforced against women. Thus, Your Honor's prepared verdict of guilty is based solely on the premise that a woman, not a man, exercised the citizen's right to vote in a political election. However, only yesterday the same manmade forms of law and justice declared it a criminal act, punishable by both fine and imprisonment, for men and women—for you, Your Honor, and for me of any of us—to give a cup of cold water, a crust of bread, or a night's shelter to a panting fugitive as he attempted to reach Canada. And you and I both know, and it is now a matter of public record, that every man, woman, and child that possessed even the faintest drop of human sympathy violated that law without regard to the terrible consequences of their actions, and these men and women were praised for their actions despite the fact that they were criminal. As then, the slaves who got their freedom had to learn to live with it and use it to undo unjust laws and procedures, so now, women must seek to find the sympathetic citizens, to gain their freedom and, with it, access to their full potential and civil rights. Women must get their right to a voice in, and to participation in, this government. I have sought to gain access to my political and civil rights, and I will seek to get these rights at every possible opportunity, regardless of the consequences. I am a woman and I will not suffer just because I am a woman!

Judge Dauber: The court will not allow the prisoner to continue! It has heard more than enough of this protest! The court orders the prisoner to sit down immediately!

Miss Waldrop [*Refusing to sit down*]: When it was announced that I would be brought to this particular court and that my trial was to be heard before Your Honor, I had high hopes that the Constitution and its recent amendments would be interpreted broadly and liberally and that this court would see that the rights of all citizens are theirs regardless of sex. I had hopes that this court would declare all citizens of these United States under its protective aegis. I had hoped that this court would declare that civil and political rights were extended to all citizens and that the courts were to protect and guarantee these rights equally to all citizens. What I had hoped for is not to be fulfilled. I have failed to receive real justice, the justice guaranteed me and all citizens under the Constitution. I have failed even to receive a trial by a jury that included men and women, both of whom are my peers. Since I have failed, I do not ask the court for leniency or forgiveness; rather, I ask the court to deal with me with the full rigor of the law and of justice.

Judge Dauber: Miss Waldrop, I must insist that you . . .
[*prisoner now sits down. A few seconds pass to allow the courtroom to settle down.*]
The court orders the prisoner to stand up to hear the verdict of the jury.
[*Miss Waldrop slowly stands, her face revealing no emotion.*]
The court finds the prisoner guilty as charged. The sentence of the court is that the prisoner pay the required fine of $150 and the costs of the prosecution.

The Prisoner Will Stand Up

WORKSHEET

If you were Miss Waldrop, which would you do?

1. Recognize the court's authority and the judge's decision and pay the $150 and additional court costs.
2. Appeal the decision on the grounds that exclusion of women citizens from voting denies them the citizenship rights guaranteed by the Constitution.
3. Refuse to pay the court costs and the $150 fine to find out what further steps the court would take against you.
4. Pay the $150 and prosecution fees while making a public statement that you do not accept the court's decision but that payment will free you to continue your work for women's rights.
5. Appeal the decision on the grounds that you were denied due process of law as guaranteed by the Constitution because you were not tried by a jury of your peers.

Of the five choices, the best would be to:

____

____

To argue that this is the best choice, one would say:

____

____

____

The Prisoner Will Stand Up

Discussion Starters

1. What worries you the most about the decision you have just made?
2. On what values did you base your decision?
3. What consequences were risked as a result of your decision?
4. What would have been the worst choice for you to have made?
5. Were most women of the late 1800s and early 1900s as concerned or as anxious to gain the franchise as Miss Waldrop?
6. Whom would you compare Miss Waldrop to in the women's liberation movement today? Why?
7. To what extent was the judge in this reading "progressive"?
8. How did you feel as the judge pronounced his sentence? Would you have felt different if the defendent had been a black man?
9. If Miss Waldrop had solicited your support for her defense, what would have been your position?

Agents of Progress

15. Agents of Progress

TEACHER PREPARATION

1. **Secure copies of the social and scientific context for each student, or choose some other means of presenting the background information leading up to the forced-choice situation.**
2. **Decide how you want to discuss the students' responses to the forced-choice situation.**
3. **Prepare a list of discussion starters.**
4. **Consider following this activity with role-playing. Identify students to play the roles of Mrs. Johnson, the boy, and the girl, and ask that they react to the alternatives presented in the forced-choice situation.**
5. **Have some students bring information to class pertaining to the legal rights of persons seeking a room in a guest house and of those operating such facilities.**

Social and Scientific Context

Mrs. Johnson has spent nearly all her life just outside the small rural community of Mascot. Her parents moved to the area when she was five and she has lived nowhere else for the last sixty-three years. Her travel has always been within a small radius of Mascot. She prides herself on not having left the county in more than two decades.

As one might expect, her limited travel has cost her friends she might have had outside the immediate area. Many of her close relatives have gradually become more distant, as she has refused to travel to see them and has always insisted that they travel to visit her. As the years have passed, her group of friends in the local community has grown to include most of her neighbors. She has grown old, content with her friends and her way of life. She has loved her community and the adjoining countryside. In turn, she has come to be well liked and respected by local townspeople and especially by her neighbors.

Mrs. Johnson's only contact with the outside world is through television news programs. The news she receives stresses such matters as ecological destruction, riots, crime, and war. Mrs Johnson refers to such events and concerns as "progress." She herself is against progress. She does not want things to change. She wants to hold fast to the good life she is leading, and she often expresses the hope that others in the next generation will live their lives as she has lived hers.

She is upset by the growth of cities and their expanding suburbs. News concerning urban sprawl and its destructive nature terrifies her. She believes that cities are dangerous and immoral because they do nothing to improve life or to help individuals, and, in fact, they corrupt the individual. The suburbs, she feels, are no more to be desired than cities. She realizes, however, that Mascot will soon be under in influence and control of some city. Furthermore, she believes that the town is seeking to enlarge itself, to expand its limits, to build its own suburbs, and to pursue progressive and hence evil goals. She tells friends that one day the citizens of Mascot will find themselves engaged in a life-and-death struggle with the city. She hopes she will not live to see this day, but plans to face it courageously should it come in her lifetime.

One thing that especially irritates Mrs. Johnson is the unrest and trouble generated by "agents of progress." To her, agents of progress are student militants, hippies, religious freaks, and drug poppers and shooters who live in the cities. She feels that the younger generation is demanding access to too many adult rights and privileges without accepting the concomitant responsibilities. Too many adults are too free in their treatment of these "agents." Under threats of crime, trouble, and riots, they give in to the demands of these assorted youth groups.

Mrs. Johnson uses every opportunity to inform her friends that she trusts no one under thirty years of age. The young, the hippie freaks, the dope pushers, the free lovers, and even the liberal city folk are certainly unlikely to receive much sympathy from her. In effect, Mrs. Johnson is a person likely to be intolerant of strangers, urbanites, and persons under thirty.

As the population of the cities has advanced into the suburbs and into the rural communities, Mrs. Johnson has become more and more vocal in her displeasure and discontent regarding the people who have begun to move into and to build in the Mascot area. However, until recently, she had not been forced to deal with any of these persons, especially the real troublemakers, her "agents of progress," who spell certain trouble.

For twenty years she helped her husband run a boarding house. Since his death, eight years ago, she has found the boarding house to be a heavy burden on her energies but realizes it is her sole source of income. Recently, new apartment houses in the town have drained off many of her boarders. She has found it difficult to find anyone to stay with her.

But last night Mrs. Johnson was faced with a dilemma. In the middle of a cloudburst, someone knocked on the door of her vacant boarding house. She opened it to welcome her new guests.

"Have you a vacant room?" she was asked.

Mrs. Johnson stared at the couple who stood, dripping wet, on her porch. The boy, looking not much older than twenty-one, was dressed in sandles, patched jeans, and a body shirt. The girl, about sixteen or seventeen, was barefoot, was dressed in ill-fitting coveralls, and was obviously pregnant. When Mrs. Johnson made inquiries, she found that the couple was not married, that the boy had no steady job, that the girl was a runaway, and that both had experimented with marijuana. Obviously, they were "agents of progress."

Mrs. Johnson, in her initial shock, could only think of four possible courses of action. These were:

1. To accept the couple on the condition that the girl contact her parents and inform them of her plight.
2. To accept the couple in hopes that she would be able to improve the girl's morals and thereby give the unborn child a "decent" mother.
3. To accept the pair because she would be legally forced to rent to them, but to require that immediate arrangements be made for a marriage in order to make the child legitimate.
4. To accept the couple on the basis of their obvious need for friendship and understanding but on the condition that the girl wear clothes befitting an expectant mother.

The course of action I would most prefer Mrs. Johnson to have taken is:

____

____

____

____

If asked to justify my choice, I would say:

____

____

____

____

____

Discussion Starters

1. What were Mrs. Johnson's opinions of the city?
2. Who were her "agents of progress"?
3. How did Mrs. Johnson associate her "agents of change" with progress?
4. Mrs. Johnson connected progress with crime, riots, wars, and environmental destruction. In what ways might she have been right? Wrong?
5. Describe the couple who appeared at the door of the boarding house.
6. How do you think Mrs. Johnson felt when the boy and girl appeared at the door?
7. How do you think the boy and girl felt while they were being interrogated by Mrs. Johnson? After the interrogation?
8. The right to privacy is one of our most precious rights. In what ways did Mrs. Johnson violate that right when she sought information from the boy and girl?
9. In what ways could Mrs. Johnson justify her need to know?

PROTOCOLS

The value sheets contained in this chapter stress the four components of the forced-choice format:

1. A problematic situation related to the unit theme, topic, or concept.
2. A limited number of options.
3. A decision sheet for students to complete.
4. A set of questions or discussion starters.

The teacher wishing to develop value sheets in the forced-choice format should:

1. Clearly state the topic, idea, or theme being taught and with which the value sheet is to be related.
2. Locate a source (magazine article, novel or short story plot, historical incident, and so forth) or contrive a situation that describes a problem relevant to the topic, idea, or theme being studied.
3. Frame and make a list of three to five possible reactions to the problematic situation, making sure that these reactions are homogeneous (that all are cast as consequences, as policies, as criteria, or as feelings).
4. Check to ensure that the choices are either all good or all bad (all attractive or all unattractive).
5. Develop a decision sheet on which students must list their choice and identify their basis for making the choice.
6. Prepare a list of discussion starters (consistent with the comprehension, relational, and valuation phases of value clarification) to help guide the follow-up discussion.
7. Consider how he or she will handle the transition from this activity in the instructional unit to the next.

Following the procedures listed above, teachers should be able to develop value sheets in the *forced-choice* format that they can incorporate into their own classroom units. Using the same knowledge, they can select and adapt value sheets already available to fit their purposes and to meet the needs of their students.

CHAPTER FIVE

THE AFFIRMATIVE FORMAT OF THE VALUE SHEET

The affirmative format of the value sheet stresses practical aspects of decision making. This format helps students to learn that the situation in which a decision must be made tends to influence how the decision is made as well as the decision itself. This format provides students with an opportunity to practice and refine their ability to empathize. The affirmative format also enables students to become aware of their freedom to invent new alternatives in order to make critical decisions, even though it may appear at first glance that no satisfactory decision is possible. The thrust of affirmative valuing exercises is the invention of alternatives for persons trapped in awkward circumstances.

The affirmative format differs from the forced-choice format in three ways. First, whereas the forced-choice format requires students to select what they believe another person or group ought to do, the affirmative format encourages students to select what *they* would do if they were another person. Second, whereas the forced-choice format requires students to provide a reason for their choice, the affirmative format may or may not ask a student to justify his response. Finally, whereas the forced-choice format provides a restricted number of options, one of which students must choose, the affirmative format suggests two or three possible alternatives but leaves students free to invent their own preferences and values as well.

The affirmative format consists of four major components: (1) a problematic situation that can be connected with an instructional unit that is being taught; (2) an awkward situation in which an individual must make a critical decision; (3) space in which a student can state what he would do if he were the person caught up in the situation; and (4) a set of discussion starters emphasizing the comprehension, relational, and valuation phases of value clarification. Some affirmative formats also provide space in which a student can explain how he would justify his decision.

The problematic situation contains sufficient information to enable the student to orient himself within the social and scientific context in which the decision is to be made. This situation should contain ways by which students can seek out relationships between the valuing situation and their knowledge of the unit being studied. The situation must clearly communicate the constraints within which a decision is to be made and must also contain adequate information for students to evaluate the congruence between their decisions and the situation within which they are operating. These situations can be contrived by the teacher, can be based on actual historical events, or can be centered on themes found in various forms of literature.

Once the problematic situation has been developed, a person (the first component) with whom students are to empathize is introduced and his position (social status), commitments, and desires are described. At this point some discrepant or unexpected event (the second component) forces the person to make a decision that is relevant to, yet limited by, constraints of the situation.

Making this decision is awkward for the individual, given his nature and background. This decision may be so because all apparent options lead to unacceptable consequences, because the individual must respond with insufficient time to organize a response, or because any decision he makes is likely to cause him to engage in behavior that violates basic beliefs he holds about himself.

At this point, a third component is introduced that requires a response from students using the value sheet. Typically, this element is introduced by an incomplete sentence of the nature: "Given the limitations of my situation, the best thing that I can do is . . ." After concluding this sentence, students may be asked to describe how they reasoned in order to arrive at their decision.

Follow-up questions continue to be important in this format of the value sheet. Comprehension, relational, and valuing questions should be carefully considered. Usually, it is better to wait until students have committed themselves before focusing their attention on these questions.

SAMPLES

Seven examples of the affirmative format are provided in this section. The reader may wish to pay close attention to the devices used to place individuals in difficult decision situations. In addition, the reader should attempt to identify each component of the affirmative format in the samples that follow.

16. Professional Desire

TEACHER PREPARATION

1. **Secure sufficient copies of the situation for each student, or ask a person who reads well to help develop an audio cassette to play.**
2. **Read your students a description of Huntington's chorea that describes the disease's cause, stages, and effects.**
3. **Decide whether you will have students share their personal letters with one another in small groups or as part of a class discussion.**
4. **Determine if you are willing to spend more than one to two days focusing on this value sheet. If you are, consider (a) distributing and discussing a table of inherited diseases, including their causes, descriptions, and effects; and (b) having different groups of students role-play the reaction of Richard's wife and his father's two friends to the different decisions reached by Richard.**

Social and Scientific Context

Dr. Richard Layne is a compassionate man, anxious to provide his fellow man with the social benefits of new medical knowledge. As a high-school biology student he became aware of and developed an intense interest in the field of inherited diseases. With further undergraduate work and medical training, his interest deepened, and he became more sensitive to the pain and suffering some individuals are doomed to bear from birth. After completing his medical training, Dr. Layne chose to pursue further studies in order to become a specialist and researcher in the area of inherited diseases.

Once Dr. Layne entered practice, he quickly established a reputation as an able doctor and a brilliant organizer. Soon he found it possible to obtain both private and foundation support for a clinic. Although he applied for public grant moneys, his applications were rejected because his clinic focused on the application of medical knowledge rather than on research. Unable to obtain public moneys to augment private and foundation gifts, and faced with inflationary costs of operating, the clinic lived a precarious existence because of inadequate operating moneys.

To support his clinic, Dr. Layne found himself spending more and more time speaking to private groups and organizations. Eventually, his speeches took on a pattern in which he stressed three themes.

The first theme was that the clinic had a social mission to perform. This mission, Dr. Layne explained, was to analyze the genes of prospective parents to determine whether they possessed genetic traits likely to adversely affect their offspring. Once it had been determined that potentially dangerous traits were present, he continued, the clinic offered counseling services. During counseling, prospective parents were informed of the risks involved should a defective child be born and they were urged to consider alternatives. When parents were willing or when they succumbed to this urging, the available alternatives were clearly spelled out and explored. During this phase of his speech, Dr. Layne outlined the work of his clinic for the laymen whose support he sought.

The second theme presented by the doctor was the potential pain, suffering, and deformity attributable to parental decisions to have children in spite of accurate genetic analysis and prognostication. At this point Dr. Layne sought to justify the direct nature with which his counselors urged genetically unfit parents to consider alternatives to conceiving children: "Any genetically unfit person who knowingly and willingly gives birth to children, and thus risks condemning them to suffering a hereditary disease or deformity, ought to be condemned and sentenced to spend an eternity in the hottest fires of hell." During this part of his speech Dr. Layne sought to proselytize the citizens to whom he spoke and win monetary pledges with which to continue his work.

Dr. Layne's third theme was the dire needs of the clinic. He outlined his difficulty in obtaining and keeping the services of a qualified staff. He described equipment and facilities that would increase the scope and social benefit of his clinic. He confessed that current circumstances had created a situation in which his clinic was barely surviving on a day-to-day basis and that its sudden demise at any moment would not be surprising.

Donations procured by this means trickled in at a rate necessary to keep the clinic in existence. But just barely.

Although he never referred to the matter publicly, Dr. Layne was particularly frustrated by the fact that his retired and reclusive father was quite a wealthy man. Moreover, his father frequently donated large sums, often in excess of $10,000, to charitable causes and was considered a humanitarian. And shortly before Richard had graduated from medical school, his father had founded the Layne Foundation and funded it with a $3 million endowment to be used to ease human suffering and improve the quality of American life. However, his father refused to donate money to the Layne Clinic and instructed the officers of the Layne Foundation to refuse all requests from the Layne Clinic, regardless of merit.

Before he became almost hermitlike in his life style, Dr. Layne's father made remarks about the Layne Clinic. He referred to it as "that thing of Richard's." He periodically hinted that the clinic was evil. He suggested that the clinic's chief effect was to cause men and women to hate and distrust one another because of a fear that their mates might possess undesirable genes. But Dr. Layne's father limited his comments to short remarks; he consistently refused to elaborate or explore his meaning with his son.

When Dr. Layne married Anne, one of the nurses who worked at the Layne Clinic, he and his wife determined that they would not have children of their own until such time that the clinic was more adequately funded. This, they felt, would enable both to continue working and would relieve some of the financial strain under which the clinic operated. They did not discuss their decision with Richard's father because he had been away for five years and had rejected a wedding invitation. Furthermore, he had requested that Richard and his new bride live their own life and allow him to do the same. He wished them good luck, sent his blessings, but made it clear that he would not welcome the company of Richard and his wife.

Three years passed, during which the clinic clung to a precarious existence. For eight years Richard had not seen his father, and for almost three years he had neither spoken with him nor received a letter from him. Then one night he was awakened by his father's lawyer and was informed that his father had died in a flaming plane crash.

Only four people attended the private burial service of Dr. Layne's father: George Kirkpatrick, Mr. Layne's confidential adviser, personal friend, and chairman of the board of the Layne Foundation; John Herman, family friend and chief legal adviser to Mr. Layne and the foundation; Richard; and his wife, Anne. Following the funeral, these four people returned to Richard's home, where John Herman read Mr. Layne's will and handed Richard a letter from his father.

For purposes of your assignment, you need not be concerned with the details of the will other than to know that George Kirkpatrick and John Herman were personally loyal to Mr. Layne and legally responsible to carry out his last will and testament. The letter from Mr. Layne to Richard presents you with your problem. The letter read:

Dear Richard:

Little did you know that I am one of those you have publicly and often chose to "condemn to hell and eternal fire." You see, Richard, I am the victim of a hereditary disease, Huntington's chorea, and my life as a recluse these past few years has been my punishment. You are doomed to the same future. There is no cure. I could not tell you this while I lived, for reasons that I hope you will understand and appreciate.

One thing you must understand is my strong sense of family obligation. I am vitally concerned that *you* have a son to continue the line of Laynes. The Layne family line has existed for countless centuries. It has enjoyed a rich and colorful history. The family has contributed much, as have you, to the improvement of man's life on this earth. To the degree that I can exercise power from beyond the grave, I will not have the Layne tradition end with you. I am bound by my forefathers, and by my own sense of duty, to do everything to preserve the Layne family line.

Therefore, I have done what I had to do.

I have instructed my lawyer, John Herman, and the chairman of the Layne Foundation, George Kirkpatrick, to carry on the work of the Layne Foundation. As you no doubt know, the Layne Foundation now has a new endowment in excess of $3 million. All my stock is to be sold (estimated value, $15 million) and is to be added to the current endowment of the foundation at my death. For five years, John and George are to continue the current program of the foundation. At the end of five years from the date of my death, they are to exercise one of two options: (1) If you should conceive a son who reaches the age of thirty months, they are to turn the foundation over to you, with its entire endowment to use as you see fit. (2) If no son is born or attains the age of thirty months within the five-year period, the energies of the foundation are to be redirected to fight the existence of clinics such as yours. The rationale for this behavior will be to save others the anguish that I have suffered because I *knew* that I carried and transmitted the disease in my genetic structure.

The decision is yours. I hope that you find it easier to wrestle with your conscience than I have found it to wrestle with mine. Regardless of your final decision, I have loved you deeply and am proud of the way you have maintained the family tradition.

Love,
Dad

Both Richard and his wife were shocked and dismayed by the letter. Richard discussed his situation with John Herman, who told him that he believed Mr. Layne's will could not be broken. He also discussed the matter with George Kirkpatrick, who tried to help Richard understand his father's ambition to maintain the family line. Finally, he discussed the matter with his wife, full of remorse that they had neglected to submit to genetic analysis prior to marriage. Following this long and often emotional discussion, Richard indicated that he would inform George and John of his decision by letter within the week. George and John left.

That evening, unable to sleep under the weight of an unmade decision, Richard decided to make his decision once and for all. In his opinion, he made the best, the only, and the ethically correct decision demanded of him as a son, doctor, administrator, humanitarian, and husband. He then drafted a letter to John Herman, his father's lawyer. The letter stated his decision and explained his reasons for having so decided. That decision was . . .

Now it's your turn. Write the letter to John Herman that Richard wrote.

Discussion Starters

1. If you had been Richard's wife, Anne, how would you have helped him to make his decision?
2. If you had been either George or John, how could you have justified destroying the will?
3. Would you refer to Mr. Layne as a moral or immoral man? Explain your answer.
4. Can Richard make a scientific decision that is not antihumanitarian? Explain your answer.
5. Can Richard make a humanitarian decision that is not antiscientific? Explain your answer.
6. Should wills such as Mr. Layne's be upheld in courts? Explain your answer.

17. School's Out

TEACHER PREPARATION

1. **Secure adequate copies of the value sheet for each student.**
2. **Encourage each student to vote privately before initiating discussions.**
3. **Determine how you will help students relate this activity to the unit you are teaching.**

Social and Scientific Context

The Japanese defeated the Russians during the Russo-Japanese War, 1904-1905. President Teddy Roosevelt received the Nobel prize for negotiating the Treaty of Portsmouth that ended this war. The Taft-Katsura executive agreement of 1905 confirmed United States' recognition of Japanese sovereignty over Korea.

Meanwhile, in California, 500 to 1,000 Japanese immigrants were coming to San Francisco annually. The combination of Chinese and Japanese immigrants comprised a small, but potentially dangerous threat to the nation, or so Californians believed. The efforts of William Randolph Hearst's newspapers intensified emotional fear of a growing "yellow peril."

You are a member of the San Francisco Public School Board. It is October 1906. You are up for re-election next month. You are attending the regular board meeting. In a surprise move, you are asked to vote on the adoption of a proposed board policy ordering the segregation of Oriental children in San Francisco. If adopted, the policy is to take effect immediately. You request a postponement of two weeks before the final vote so that you can investigate the matter and study the facts. However, your motion for postponement is defeated by a 3-2 vote. You realize that in a few minutes you will have to vote on whether to exclude all Oriental children from all public schools in the city. In the few minutes before you have to vote, you quickly consider these points:

1. You are committed to providing the best education for *all* children, regardless of ethnic origin and sex.
2. A negative vote will jeopardize your political future.
3. You are personally alarmed at the increasing military strength of the Japanese.
4. You perceive possible ramifications in terms of future exclusion of other minority groups.
5. An affirmative vote will not be accepted or understood by your Oriental laundress, by your children's Oriental playmates, or by your children.
6. If you vote affirmatively, members of the Niagra Movement (the civil rights organization that preceded the NAACP) to which you belong will find it difficult to accept your sincerity.
7. The president of the corporation where you are employed is actively supporting the exclusion of Oriental children from the public school his children attend.
8. Your last election was won without the support of the Hearst newspapers.
9. Your church (where you are a deacon) is on record as supporting equal education for Oriental children.

The board finishes its discussion and debate. You gaze around the meeting room. It is unusually "packed" for a regular meeting of the board, but there are no Orientals present. The Hearst newspapers are well represented, despite their usual practice of having only one reporter attend. The audience is anxiously anticipating the decision of the school board.

The time has arrived for a voice vote, and, in accordance with the rotation system being employed, *you* are to vote first. When your name is called you vote: ______Yes ______No.

If pushed by a voter to justify your decision, you would say:

____

____

____

____

____

Discussion Starters

1. When you realized you would soon have to vote, you considered a number of points. Which points moved you to vote as you did? Which points did you ignore?
2. List the consequences you will have to live with as a result of your decision.
3. If you were faced with this sort of decision, what would your feelings be?
4. One frequently hears that those elected to represent others should carry out the wishes of their constituents. To what degree is this possible? Is this a good ideal or a bad one?
5. Officeholders swear to uphold the Constitution. Furthermore, they are expected to follow this ideal. How might the ideal of representing voters and that of upholding the Constitution come into conflict?
6. If you were faced with a conflict between these ideals, which would you choose to support?

UNIVERSITY
CLUB
What a tremendous
practical joke...
what style...
AVONDALE
5 MILES

18. The Price of Loyalty

TEACHER PREPARATION

1. **Secure sufficient copies of the value sheet for each student who will participate in the activity.**
2. **Decide how you will group students for the activity.**
3. **Adjust the discussion starters in order to make the value sheet consistent with the content you are studying at the time you assign it.**

Social and Scientific Context

As a university freshman, you are on your way home for the Halloween weekend. As you drive east toward your home at twilight, the headlights of your car pick up a roadside sign:

AVONDALE 5 miles

The sign jogs your memory and you begin to recall newspaper stories that you have read and news accounts that you have heard about the town of Avondale.

Avondale, you remember, is a town of about 15,000 persons nestled in a peaceful valley. Because of its beautiful natural setting, the nearness of the university, and an availability of services for the elderly, Avondale has become a retirement community. Until twelve months ago, the town of Avondale had never made the front page of the city newspapers. Within the last twelve months, however, the town has been quite newsworthy.

First, in October and November of last year, heavy winter rains led to a major flood in the valley where Avondale is situated. In spite of some advance warning, damage to property was heavy and a dozen persons were drowned. Of the dozen persons who drowned, five were over sixty. The remainder of those who lost their lives were in their twenties and thirties.

Since the flood, the town has been cleaned up and, on the surface, few signs of the flood remain. Nevertheless, psychiatrists and mental health personnel who work with the elderly of Avondale have reported that the elderly live with a constant anxiety that they will die in the next flood. Psychiatrists have also reported that many of the elderly become more frightened instead of being reassured when they are presented with the facts. The facts are:

1. The flood of last year was the first known case of Avondale experiencing a flood in which a human life was lost.
2. Most of the persons who drowned in the flood were not elderly.
3. The meterological conditions that led to the abnormal rains and flood are not likely to recur.
4. Emergency measures have now been designed and tested by which it would be possible to evacuate Avondale residents prior to flooding should the same conditions reoccur.

In spite of this information, the retired people, living in comfortable houses, possessing the necessary resources to live out their lives happily, and having every reason to feel secure, are by and large very frightened.

Most of your knowledge of the flood and consequent fear are based on news accounts and newspaper stories you heard and read last winter. But during the last three weeks Avondale has once again become newsworthy, this time as the focus of a number of flying saucer reports.

During the first week of October, a man and his wife reported an unidentified flying object to the sheriff's office. By the end of the week, a deputy sheriff on late night patrol and a number of workers driving home between 10:00 and 12:00 P.M. had reported mysterious flying objects with flashing lights in the sky over Avondale.

By the second and third weeks of October, rumors were running rife. An elderly man and his wife who were driving to Avondale were yanked, car and all, into the sky and disappeared without a trace. A local citizen, known to enjoy a pause at the bar before going home, ran his car into a ditch. Arrested for drunk driving and fined, he complained that a lighted object had swept down from the sky and that in order to avoid a head-on collision he had taken to the ditch. The death of a hitchhiker had been officially listed as a hit-and-run accident, but many reported that he looked as though he had been tortured and dropped from the sky. A nearby farmer lost some of his herd of cattle; while the sheriff spoke of rustlers, many Avondale residents insisted that the cattle had been taken by strange beings from another world in an alien spaceship. A local fortuneteller reported that all astrological signs pointed to an imminent invasion of Earth, with Avondale being the most logical initial conquest. Immediately, persons who had never placed much value in astrology become confident that she was right in her prediction.

Not surprising then, Avondale is tense. The elderly are near the point of panic, and their nervousness has made other residents anxious.

Psychologists have sought to allay fears and relieve tension by offering a logical explanation for the rumors: Residents of the town live in constant fear and have so lived for twelve months. Nothing whatsoever in the facts of their life justifies this terror. So in order to explain their unreasonable fear, residents of Avondale have manufactured rumors about flying saucers. By believing in the flying saucers and accepting the truth of rumors, the fear they feel can be made reasonable and acceptable. This explanation, however, has proven ineffective in curbing fear and relieving anxiety. Fear, tension, and near panic continue to prevail.

As you climb the long, steep grade toward the top of the ridge from which you will be able to spot Avondale, you chuckle and treasure your recollections. Your mood is interrupted by the flashing of an indicator that means your engine is overheated. You pull to the side of the road, stop your engine, and raise the hood so that the engine will cool. Knowing that you will need to wait about thirty minutes, you notice an old logging road leading toward the valley and decide to take a short exploratory walk to pass the time.

You walk for about a hundred yards, enjoying the brisk mountain air and admiring the stars shining in a cloudless sky. Then, rounding a turn in the road, you almost bump into a large panel truck. Examining the truck more carefully, you discover that it belongs to a popular coeducational club sponsored by your university. You are positive in your identification for you have visited the clubhouse and have often seen the closed truck on campus. In addition, the sides and rear of the truck contain the symbolic decal of the club. Finding the truck arouses your curiosity, and discovering that it belongs to the university club only intensifies your original interest. After all, this is the club that you hope you will be invited to join before the year is out. You have already done all that you can do to seek membership, and you are awaiting an invitation that is by no means certain to be forthcoming. However, you are hopeful.

Just as you are about to wander further down the old logging road, you hear a group of people moving toward you, whispering and laughing. You decide to hide in the brush and to determine who is sharing the old logging road with you. Almost immediately a group of young men and women wearing windbreakers you associate with the campus club return to the van. You can tell that they are sharing past successes and anticipating still another triumph.

While you observe, the group opens the read doors of the van and begins to remove objects. One boy removes a small box that looks like a transistor radio and extends an antenna. A girl removes a backpack from the van and helps the boy fasten the pack on his back. Together, the boy and the girl connect the "radio" to the pack with what appear to be electrical wires. Two other students lift a flat, oblong object from the van and tinker with it. Despite the absence of light, the group works efficiently, indicating much prior experience with the equipment. With the equipment checked, two boys carry the oblong object, which you notice is topped with two propellers, back down the road, followed by other members of the group. In order to satisfy your curiousity, you stalk the group.

Members of the group move to a clearing from which the lights of Avondale are barely visible, and they place the oblong object on the ground. The young man with the backpack begins to play with the black box that had appeared to be a transistor radio. Four events then occur: (1) flashing lights illuminate the object placed in the clearing and make it look like an elliptical circle; (2) the propellers on the object begin to turn and to lift the object, now blinking wildly, into the air; (3) the object begins to emit a low wailing noise; and (4) the object floats out over the valley and toward the town of Avondale. You realize that you have watched the successful launching of a flying saucer.

Your immediate reaction is delight. What a tremendous practical joke! What style! Imagine the creativity of the club, the success of the Halloween project! Beyond a doubt, the belief that this is the club you should join is confirmed.

After about thirty minutes, the flying saucer lands. Not wishing to be detected and cast in the role of a spy, you hastily return to your car and drive into the outskirts of Avondale, where you are stopped by a roadblock. A civilian wearing a civil defense armband informs you that you may proceed through town cautiously, at your own risk, if you wish.

Anxious as to why you can only proceed at your own risk, you turn on your radio. You discover that the latest flying saucer has caused a severe panic. A score of heart attacks have been attributed to the latest reported sightings. At least two couples are reported to have committed suicide rather than to risk capture and torture by aliens from outer space. A number of elderly persons attempting to flee have been involved in automobile accidents, some of which have been fatal. Looting is reported in the shopping center. Local police, unable to control the town, have requested and are awaiting the assistance of the state national guard. You are dismayed. You hardly know what to do.

You attempt to weigh the consequences of alternative actions carefully. If you report what you know:

- Your efforts to get home will be delayed an undeterminable amount of time.
- The news may help calm the panic-stricken population and save lives.
- The news may mean the end of the university club and most certainly will kill whatever chances you had of joining.

If you fail to report what you saw:

- You will protect your friends at the university who certainly had no intention other than to engage in a practical joke.
- Further loss of life, for which you may be held responsible, is likely.

You consider these choices quickly, for an immediate decision is demanded. Having considered, you make up your mind. You decide to do the best and the only thing that you could do in this situation. Your decision is to . . .

Discussion Starters

1. What were the conditions that existed in Avondale as you proceeded to drive through the community?
2. Under what conditions does one abandon his own age group in favor of his concern for those in another age group? Provide examples.
3. In some ways, it might be claimed that the university club members were taking advantage of the fears and anxieties of the citizens of Avondale. Is it good or bad for persons to take advantage of the fears and anxieties of another group of people? Explain.
4. Are there times when manipulating the fears and anxieties of another group of people can be good? Cite examples to support your answer.
5. The sightings of objects such as the Loch Ness monster, the abominable snowman, and flying saucers may be described as "figments of imagination." What objects found in the literature and arts of past societies and cultures might be described as figments of their imagination? Explain.
6. In what ways might real events be distorted by one's imagination? Can one's imagination be distorted by accurate data?
7. Some people firmly believe that flying saucers have landed, and are still landing, on Earth and that these saucers are manned by aliens from other planets. What are your attitudes and feelings toward those persons who claim to have been taken aboard these alien spaceships?

19. Tender Loving Care

TEACHER PREPARATION

1. **Explain how videotape is used to make a visual and verbal record of what occurs. If necessary, use the analogy of a tape recorder.**
2. **Define the concept of terminal illness.**
3. **Review or teach the Hippocratic oath.**
4. **Secure a copy of the value sheet for each student who will participate in the value clarification activity.**
5. **Decide whether you wish students to work individually or in small groups.**

Social and Scientific Context

You have spent a long and dreary night watching videotape replays of hospital patients assigned to an experimental section of University Hospital. As a doctor and as a teacher who is involved in the training of doctors, nurses, and other health-related personnel, you are studying the care and treatment of patients who are known to be dying. You have three primary goals:

1. To analyze and describe the problems peculiar to the care and treatment of the terminally ill.
2. To identify areas in which the care and treatment of the terminally ill can and should be improved.
3. To select instances in which doctors, nurses, and other health-related personnel exhibit behaviors that are models of how the terminally ill should be cared for and treated.

In order to avoid interfering with the work of doctors and others, you have placed television cameras and videotape decks in the rooms of patients who have agreed to be videotaped. This enables you to study how the terminally ill are treated. Videotaping also enables you to store models of how the terminally ill should be treated. Tapes not useful as models are erased and reused to cut research expenses.

Already today you have watched more than five hours of tape. You have carefully observed the responses of a dozen dying persons to the acts of nurses, doctors, practical nurses, and orderlies. In so doing, you have witnessed pain, hoplessness, despair, and dignity. You have seen how truly cowardly as well as how bravely a person can face his ultimate fate. As difficult as these five hours have been for you, you have dreaded the tape that you must now analyze. This tape is labeled innocently enough:

John (Johnny) Paul Greene
Age: 14
Leukemia: terminal
Research code number: 1041

You know that this tape will be the most trying one for you. Whereas up to now you have been watching persons past the prime of life die, you must now watch a young person's last minutes of life. Today Johnny Greene died.

As you remove the videotape from its container and thread the videotape deck, you remember Johnny. Only a month ago he was admitted, when it was discovered that he had a severe case of leukemia. At first doctors believed that Johnny would live for several months, perhaps for a few years. However, his condition rapidly deteriorated, and his doctor's prognosis was changed to read several days, perhaps a few weeks at most. In addition, Johnny was found to be allergic to those medicines most effective at easing his pain. By the end of his second week at the hospital, Johnny had accepted the fact that he would soon be dead.

As Johnny's condition worsened, he was placed on the terminal floor. With his parents' permission, you began monitoring his treatment and care. You recall that machines were constantly being used to provide his body with life-prolonging fluids. Johnny did not complain about his experiences as part of a mechanized life-support system. When he had moments without pain, he cherished talking with others, and his smile was both contagious and radiant. Between these moments his frail body sometimes writhed in pain, but he did not blame his suffering on others. Indeed, he still managed to have a smile and a kind word for his favorite nurse, Mrs. Guertin. The relationship between Johnny and Mrs. Guertin has already provided you with a number of taped episodes you believe will be useful for purposes of training future doctors and nurses to care for terminally ill young persons.

Three days ago Johnny's condition became critical. Since that time, his only communication with the world had been the horrible contortions of his body and the pain etched in his face. Johnny's final hours, you realize, were hours of almost unbearable pain. Without the support of machines, he would have died rapidly. After three days, those who knew Johnny best, including you, were thankful that his suffering had been terminated by death.

With the tape threaded in your equipment, you begin viewing it. First, you hear the door to Johnny's room opening, which switches on your recording equipment. Next, you see Mrs. Guertin moving toward Johnny's bed with a clipboard in her hand. Reaching Johnny's bedside, Mrs. Guertin checks each element in the apparatus that is keeping Johnny alive, referring to a checklist held in place by the clipboard she carries. When she is finished, she strokes Johnny's forehead and rushes from the room. You observe that her affection for Johnny has made it impossible for her to keep her composure.

When Mrs. Guertin enters the room for a second time, your equipment again becomes operational. She moves to Johnny's bed. She looks quite composed as she removes a small clamp from her pocket and attaches it to one of the plastic tubes entering Johnny's body. Slipping this section of tubing under the sheet that covers Johnny's body, Mrs. Guertin kisses him and leaves the room with a trace of a smile on her face.

Immediately you turn off your replay equipment. You know that Mrs. Guertin has deliberately hastened Johnny's death. You know that her action is legally wrong. You recall your Hippocratic oath. You know that you can erase the tape and that no one will ever know what occurred. You know that if you make others aware of what you know, Mrs. Guertin may be charged with murder. You decide to do the best possible thing under these circumstances. Having made your decision, you . . .

Discussion Starters

1. What was the nature of the videotape observation system set up in the terminally ill ward of University Hospital?
2. Why were the terminally ill patients being observed and videotaped.
3. What were some of the reasons why the Johnny Greene case was so different?
4. What is leukemia? What are its symptoms? How does it affect the human body?
5. What was the nature of the relationship between Johnny Greene, patient, and Mrs. Guertin, nurse?
6. Should patient-nurse relationships be similar to or different from that of Johnny Greene and Nurse Guertin? Explain.

7. Who would most benefit from a relationship such as that between Johnny and Mrs. Guertin? Who would benefit least? State reasons for your choices.
8. What was your decision? What reasons made it the most attractive of the alternatives you had available to you?
9. How did you feel when you saw Mrs. Guertin smile after she had taken steps to terminate the life of Johnny? How do you think Nurse Guertin felt? If Johnny knew, how did he feel?

Tender Loving Care

20. Soldiers

TEACHER PREPARATION

1. **Secure copies of the social and scientific context for each student in the class.**
2. **Decide how the class will discuss their responses to the situation presented in the activity.**
3. **Prepare a list of discussion starters.**

Social and Scientific Context

Billy and Tom were lifelong friends. Everything they did was with the other in mind. They had even considered going into the ministry together but had decided against it at the last minute.

Both were happy with the way things had worked out for them in the army. They had joined the army on the "buddy system" to insure their friendship would continue. Camp Bingo was a minor supply base miles from any enemy action.

Things couldn't have been more perfect for the two.

One day, while on a routine scouting mission just outside the camp, an enemy soldier suddenly opened fire on the two and hit Billy.

Seeing Billy fall, Tom turned and saw the sniper running through the bushes. Tom aimed his rifle and pulled the trigger. No shot! His gun had jammed. He immediately started to chase the sniper.

Moments later he came upon the sniper, who lay sprawled on the grass. He had tripped over a log and had broken his leg. He began crying aloud "I surrender! I surrender! "as Tom approached.

Tom glanced over his shoulder in the direction of Billy and . . .

Discussion Starters

1. What information in the story supports the statement that Billy and Tom were friends?
2. What is the "buddy system" program that the army offers?
3. Why didn't Tom shoot the sniper immediately after he and Billy were fired upon?
4. Where does this story take place? Explain.
5. If the two soldiers were such close friends, why didn't Tom stay to help Billy rather than chase the sniper?
6. To what degree did Tom's friendship with Billy affect his decision as to what to do with the injured sniper?
7. How do you think Billy felt when Tom abandoned him to pursue the sniper? What were Tom's feelings?
8. In what ways might some methods of killing during war be considered good methods and others, bad methods? Is sniping a "good" method? Explain.

21. Nasty Questions

TEACHER PREPARATION

1. **Decide whether you wish to distribute copies of the situation to class members, to present the situation orally, or to have your students role-play the episode.**
2. **Discuss role-playing as a means of attempting to think, feel, and react as others do; stress that reactions to this sheet should be in the form of, "If I thought, felt, and acted as someone else . . ."**

Social and Scientific Context

In real life, all of us frequently find ourselves in a position in which we must explain to others why we have taken a certain stand or have engaged in a certain action. This exercise is designed to help us clarify some of the ways we react to these situations (or might react to these situations) when questions of life and death are involved and we find ourselves forced into a box of our own making. For purposes of this exercise you are to assume the following role:

1. You are opposed to laws that make it impossible for a woman to obtain an abortion.
2. You have actively participated in a campaign to make abortion legal in your state, a campaign that has not yet been successful.
3. You have been active in disseminating birth control information in your state.
4. You have actively lobbied in your state legislature for the free distribution of birth control pills and devices to welfare recipients.
5. You are part of a group that helps women seeking an abortion to make arrangements in states that you consider to be more enlightened about this matter than your own.
6. At the moment you are a member of a panel discussing the pros and cons of abortion before a group of nurses. You have committed yourself to the idea of legalized abortion in your state.

At this point, a nurse rises and makes the following points:

> I worked as a nurse in Honolulu. Abortion on demand is legal there. A number of nurses, including myself, have experienced severe emotional problems because they are expected to participate in abortions. After all, we are sworn to protect life and to do all we can to preserve it. We were told that this holds for *all life,* even for a premature infant, no matter how fragile or tiny it may be.
> As for myself, I left Hawaii. Even with psychiatric help I found myself going to pieces as a nurse and as a person. Once we were performing a Caesarean abortion. We opened the mother's womb and lifted out a small baby. The baby moved its arms and legs and managed one small cry. Without thinking, I snatched the baby and started for the incubator to preserve its life. I was immediately stopped and told to keep my mind on the task at hand, that this was an abortion. The baby had to die.

Having presented her experiences, the nurse scans the audience and asks you one question, "Can we live with ourselves if we permit abortion to become an acceptable medical practice in America?"

The nurse has, in effect, asked you to establish some basis (criterion) by which we can better live with ourselves if a law legalizing abortion is passed. Since you are already committed to the passage of such a law, you search your mind and develop the best single argument as to why those sworn to respect and preserve life should also participate in abortions. That argument is . . .

Discussion Starters

1. Did you feel comfortable while the nurse was making her points.
2. Did you feel comfortable responding to the nurse in setting your criterion for life and death?
3. Would you support legalized abortion if given the choice?
4. Based on this experience, what aspects of abortion would worry you the most?
5. Under what conditions, if any, would you find abortion most acceptable? Least acceptable?
6. When does a developing baby become a person, entitled to society's protection from those who would murder him?
7. During her period of training, did the nurse in this episode have adequate training in ethics? Explain.

22. In the Public Eye

TEACHER PREPARATION

1. **Secure copies of the social and scientific context for each student.**
2. **Decide whether you wish to review the situation with the students before you have them complete the assignment in order to make sure they understand the full circumstance in which they are placed.**
3. **Prepare a list of discussion starters.**
4. **Decide how you want to handle the written responses of the students to the two questions posed from the floor.**

Social and Scientific Context

For purposes of this activity, you are to act as though you are a person who has worked long and hard for a number of years to have an international airport located in your city. You have gained the support of your city officials. You have convinced members of Congress from your state that an airport is desirable. You have gained the support of officials of the Federal Aviation Agency. Both the governor of your state and the local delegation to your state legislature have promised their cooperation. When the senior Senator from your state calls and informs you that Congress has just appropriated several millions of federal dollars to enable a group to plan an international airport, you are pleased but not surprised. You had expected that your plans and hopes would soon begin to be realized.

What does surprise you is the attention and publicity that you have suddenly begun to receive. The governor has publicly acknowledged your work at a press conference. The mayor and members of the city council have passed a resolution expressing the gratitude of the city. You are interviewed, and the history of your efforts is reported by television commentators and is detailed in newspaper stories. A number of civic clubs present you with awards. Eventually, the state legislature and city officials decide to hold a banquet in your honor, with you as the featured speaker. Your speech, you are told, should be informal and should address itself to the reasons for your efforts in behalf of an international airport.

More than 2,000 persons purchase tickets to the dinner. Among the guests are the Congressional delegation from your state, officials of the Federal Aviation Agency, the mayor, members of the city government, county commissioners, a representative of the President, important members of the bar, and the editors of all the major newspapers in your state. In addition, a local television station arranges a statewide network of stations to broadcast your speech live. The people who can make the airport a reality are present, and the citizens who can influence their behavior will be able to see and hear you on television. You are to be in the public eye with a real chance to shape public opinion.

The day of the banquet arrives. You have every reason to believe that this will be the greatest public moment of your life.

The dinner is excellent. Your forty-five minute speech goes well as you informally state some of the reasons why you have worked for an international airport and recount anecdotes about your personal experiences. The audience is quite supportive. When you tell jokes, everyone laughs. When you are serious, everyone is attentive. When you refer to persons who assisted you, the audience applauds. At the conclusion of your speech, you receive a standing ovation. This is indeed an occasion you did not expect and will not forget.

Having thanked the audience for its kindness, you head for your seat. The master of ceremonies returns to the microphone. Guests begin to take their seats. However, one distinguished-looking guest continues to stand. As the applause dies away, this person approaches the master of ceremonies and requests permission to ask you a vital question in the public interest. When the master of ceremonies suggests that this is neither the time nor the place for such a question, you interrupt and ask that you be allowed to hear and respond to the gentleman's question. The master of ceremonies agrees to allow one question and introduces the man, who proceeds to express his question to you in the following manner:

> Mr. Speaker, I have been keeping myself informed as to the progress of the new international airport. I must say that I am overwhelmed by the effort and work that you have devoted to this project. I realize that you did this out of sincere public interest and not for any private gain. I share the admiration for you as a person that this audience has already expressed. But to admire your efforts and the spirit in which you have worked is not to agree with your beliefs that an international airport is desirable. Before the project is approved, citizens and leaders need to consider that an international airport will lead to a number of undesirable consequences. Among these, the following are most important:
>
> 1. An international airport would require clearing thousands of acres of land now covered with vegetation. This land would be converted into runways, buildings, driveways, parking lots, and so forth. The damage to our local ecology is beyond estimation.
> 2. An international airport would add to air pollution. Not only would the city be faced with the exhaust of airplanes, but the exhaust of service vehicles is also likely to be enormous. No method for restricting this sort of pollution is now available.
> 3. An international airport would increase the level of noise to such a high and continuous level that the danger to the hearing organs of local citizens is beyond calculation. There is evidence to suggest that such noise even affects the growing fetus in pregnant women. Evidence also suggests that psychological and emotional problems, such as anxiety, apprehension, and general nervousness, result from high levels of noise.
> 4. An international airport will cause property values in residential areas surrounding the airport, wherever it is located, to go down. This will in turn enable industries to purchase land cheaply, whereas they would have had to pay current owners a handsome price for the land. Eventually, the entire section of the county will have to be rezoned to make adjustments to the proposed airport.
> 5. An international airport would make it necessary for the city to build new highways with as many as six lanes. Current patterns of traffic congestion would be made worse, and the citizens would find themselves paying higher taxes to support the building and maintenance of ground transportation facilities.
> 6. An international airport would become a military target in the event of a major international conflict.
> 7. An international airport could easily become the focus of international violence on the part of militants. Innocent citizens would thus be asked to incur unnecessary risks to their lives.

8. An international airport would have to be policed to prevent hijacking. Hiring the necessary security personnel and equipment would again cost the taxpayers money.

Mr. Speaker, I guess I really have two questions: What advantages can you find for an international airport that outweigh these undesirable effects? Why should the citizens of this city and this state run these risks?

When the man is through talking, you realize that you have made a tactical error. You have encouraged a question before assembled political figures and in front of a statewide audience that must be answered. In addition, you must answer quickly and without hesitation. Suddenly, the future of your airport that seemed so secure hinges on your ability to respond to these two questions.

Write your response to the questioner as you would deliver it.

Discussion Starters

1. What are some of the ways the public recognized your efforts in getting the legislation passed in support of the international airport?
2. Who were some of the people attending the banquet being held in your honor?
3. In your own words, what were the major points presented by the questioner?
4. Which of the questioner's reasons did you consider to be legitimate? Illegitimate?
5. How did you respond to his reasons when you attempted to answer his two questions?
6. Suppose you ignored the ecological effects of the new airport. How might one be justified in accusing you of condemning tomorrow's children for the sake of personal gain and glory today?
7. What is the relationship between progress and ecological destruction?
8. How do you feel about persons who consistently vote for progress over ecology? For ecology over progress?

PROTOCOLS

The value sheets in this chapter emphasized four components that are usually included in the affirmative format of the value sheet. Specifically, these components are

1. A problematic situation related to the unit being studied.
2. A crucial decision-making situation that does not limit the individual to options specified in the situation.
3. A space in which students can record their response to the decision-making situation.
4. A set of questions to serve as discussion starters.

With an understanding of these four components, teachers may wish to create their own affirmative value clarification activities.

The teacher wanting to design and develop value sheets in the affirmative format should

1. Clearly state the topic, idea, or theme he is teaching and to which the value sheet is to be related.
2. Locate or identify a situation in which an individual must make a choice in terms of either the greater good or the lesser evil of several alternatives. If necessary the teacher can abstract or rewrite the situation, emphasizing specific points most relevant to his unit of study.
3. Check to ensure that an adequate amount of background information is provided to maintain some frame of reference for students.
4. Check to ensure that at least two options are apparent and real to the person making the decision, with little or no indication that he can consider and choose other options.
5. End the problematic situation by placing the student in the position of having to make a decision, and emphasize the fact that he is to make the best possible decision.
6. Provide space (and enough time) for students to examine the situation and to make their decision.
7. Prepare a set of discussion starters consistent with the comprehension, relational, and valuation phases of value clarification.
8. Consider how the transition will be made from this activity to the next in the instructional unit.

By following these procedures, teachers can develop value sheets in the affirmative format relevant to their own instructional units and to the needs of their students.

CHAPTER SIX

THE RANK-ORDER FORMAT OF THE VALUE SHEET

The rank-order format of the value sheet emphasizes a hierarchical view of preference and feelings. This format is designed to help an individual examine his values and beliefs in a manner that will allow him to realize his own internal hierarchical belief system. This format stresses the need to have students discriminate between choices in terms of relative goodness and badness, and it serves to help students examine and clarify their preferences in terms of priorities. The rank-order format provides students with the opportunity to consider an entire spectrum of values, beliefs, or feelings simultaneously and to assign priorities to the values and beliefs they hold.

As people go about the task of living in their society, they develop numerous values, beliefs, and ideas about themselves and their world. They develop strong attachments to some objects of valuation; they hold weaker desires for other objects. Whatever the degree of value one assigns to a particular object, that value becomes part of his belief system. Those elements of one's environment that are valued the most receive higher priority within the system than those elements that are valued least. The higher the value priority of an object, the more it will influence one's beliefs and his subsequent actions. As his experience grows, so do the number and complextiy of his value assignments. If a particular value is consistent with one's other values, an individual can remain consistent in his behavior. However, a person may grasp hold of, and assign high value to, ideas, ideals, and beliefs simply because one is expected to do so. A person may, then, profess a firm belief in these ideals and values and may even act, on occasion, in ways congruent with them. Because individuals may have never experienced competition between their values and beliefs, they may assign higher priority to some values than these would warrant if the individual had to consciously assign different weights to them. The person only discovers such discrepancies when he is put into a situation in which he is forced to act in ways consistent with his value priority system. The rank-order format places students in this type of situation.

The rank-order format of the value sheet consists of four elements: (1) a situation that provides sufficient background information for understanding the context in which a number of options are to be rank ordered; (2) a list of five to twelve options that are to be rank ordered; (3) a set of clear and exact directions as to how students are to rank order the options listed; and (4) a set of discussion starters likely to elicit student statements consistent with the comprehension, relational, and valuation phases of value clarification.

The first component presents a social situation in which one needs to determine his priorities. The main purposes of this component are to help students identify and become familiar with persons and circumstances that present a number of alternatives to be considered, and to suggest to students possible ramifications of the priorities they assign to different options.

The second component consists of a list of five to twelve alternatives that are to be ranked. This set of options must be homogeneous in two ways. First, the list contains a set of policies, a set of consequences, a set of interpretations, or a set of preferences. The set of options should not contain more than one of these categories of statements. Second, all options should be nearly equal in attractiveness or unattractiveness, and neutral alternatives should be avoided. The alternatives identified in the rank-order task must also fit in with the contextual background established in the first component.

The third component of the rank-order format is a set of instructions that serve to introduce students to rank-order procedures. These instructions inform the students as to how one rank orders items: "Mark the choice you like the *best* with a "1," mark your second choice with a "2," mark your third choice with a "3," and so on, until you have ranked all items." These instructions are usually presented just before the alternatives to be considered and are phrased to fit the context of the situation leading to the rank-order exercise.

The rank-order format includes a set of questions. These questions serve to help students comprehend and understand the situation to be evaluated, and they assist students in their understanding of the choices they were requested to rank. These questions enable students to identify and clarify relationships among the contextual situation, the alternatives, and the unit they are studying. These questions also aid students as they seek to examine and understand the choices they made and the grounds upon which they determined their rankings.

SAMPLES

The rank-order format of the value sheet can be designed with a great deal of flexibility. It may be written in order to incorporate consequential analysis. It may be culminated by asking students to justify the item they have ranked best or worst. The rank-order format may also be written to incorporate small-group activities directly relating to, or resulting from, the rank-order task included in the value sheet. Some of this flexibility is illustrated in the samples that follow.

23. Assembling an Economic Franchise

TEACHER PREPARATION

1. **Decide whether students are to rank order the policies presented in this task individually or as members of small groups.**
2. **Develop a set of discussion starters consistent with the unit you are teaching when this value sheet is assigned.**
3. **Review with students the function and power of members of a board of directors in a corporation.**

Social and Scientific Context

For purposes of this exercise, you are to assume that you are a member of the board of directors of a large, well-known automobile company. You and your fellow board members are discussing how large a voice, if any, the workers should be given in determining such company policies as wages, working conditions, and production.

Each member of the board of directors has been handed a list of nine possible ways that workers could be allowed to participate in company decisions. Each member, including you, has been asked to rank order these possibilities from best to worst. You are to rank order the choices from the one you believe is best (with a "1") to the one you believe is worst (with a "9"). Each member of the board is asked to keep in mind the image of the company, the volume of company sales, profits, and the history of work stoppages engaged in by workers as he rank orders the possible ways in which workers could be given a larger voice in economic policy making.

The nine possibilities that you are to rank order are:

_____ Because the workers are directly responsible for producing the automobiles and making the profits, they should make all the decisions.

_____ Each section in the factory (welders, electricians, and so forth) should elect two individuals as their representatives. All of the sectional representatives should then meet and elect one person to act as the "workers' voice." This person, once elected, would sit on the board of directors and would hold his title for as long as he is employed by the company.

_____ Each worker that has been employed with the company for three or more years should be allowed to vote on all company policies concerning wages, profits, and production.

_____ All the workers should elect one man to be their representative on the board of directors. He should make decisions for the workers based on his interpretation of developments.

_____ Management should make decisions concerning company policies; however, workers should be encouraged to express grievances and to make suggestions for the board of directors to consider.

_____ Workers who make the fewest errors and produce the most work should be allowed to participate in decision making.

_____ Each worker should have a vote with regard to policies of the company; however, the board of directors should hold a binding power to veto the results of such elections.

_____ The management should appoint two or three workers to sit with the board of directors.

_____ Since workers are paid an honest and just wage for an honest day's work, they should have no voice in the making of company policy.

Discussion Starters

1. What is your role in this value sheet?
2. With whom are you working when you rank order the policies provided?
3. Suppose you had to present and defend your list before a group of militant labor union leaders. What would your feelings be?
4. Suppose you encountered a person who believed that political policy should be determined in the same way as you believe economic policy should be made. What would you say to this person?
5. Suppose American workers were allowed to participate in the making of economic decisions. Would this weaken the profit motive in America? Would this weaken the spirit of competition between firms?
6. The worker who makes the lowest wages and performs the meanest tasks dreams of the day when he, too, will be a capitalist. To what degree is this dream a possibility? With what consequences for the working person?

24. If

TEACHER PREPARATION

1. **Secure one copy of the value sheet for each student.**
2. **Help students to explore how aircraft can be used to serve each of the purposes listed in the value sheet.**
3. **Explain how items are rank ordered in terms of preference.**
4. **Have each student rank order the purposes presented in the value sheet.**
5. **Decide whether you want students to work in small groups and attempt to arrive at a consensus. If you decide to use this option, establish the rule that unanimous decisions are to be arrived at by reason–that is, that disputes cannot be resolved by a majority vote.**

Social and Scientific Context

Following you will find a number of purposes and functions that aircraft can fulfill. Each purpose or function can be encouraged by government subsidies and by federal regulations. Each can be limited by smaller government subsidies or by tighter federal regulations. Your task is to rank these purposes of aircraft from the one you most prefer to see encouraged to the one you least prefer to see encouraged. Do so by placing a "1" by your first choice, a "2" by your second choice, and so on until you have assigned a number to each purpose.

_____ Inaccessible regions and locations are made accessible by the airplane and the helicopter. They anable remote people to participate in civilized forms of activity that their isolation would otherwise make impossible.

_____ Airplanes, space vehicles, and balloons have made it possible for man to explore the atmosphere and outer space. In addition, they have opened up new frontiers for astronomy.

_____ Aircraft have made it possible and economical for man to spread fertilizers, herbicides, and insecticides over large areas of agricultural land, thereby contributing to the productivity of the American farmer and freeing a greater number of persons to work in industrial jobs.

_____ Aircraft can be used to rush emergency goods and services into areas that experience such catastrophes as earthquakes, tornadoes, blizzards, and floods. Other aircraft can be used as ambulances to remove injured persons to hospitals for intensive care and treatment.

_____ Aircraft contribute to Americans' use of leisure time. Professional athletes, musicians, and actors move easily from place to place. A housewife in Kansas can plan to attend a Broadway play in New York. A family can save for a plane or glider and make flying a hobby.

Discussion Starters

1. How can government agencies exercise control over the use of aircraft?
2. To what degree can similar forms of activity be used to exercise control over your town or community?
3. When should governments attempt to control the behavior of men?
4. What negative consequences are likely to result from your highest ranked preference?

25. On the Edge of Objectivity

TEACHER PREPARATION

1. **Secure sufficient copies of the value sheet for each participant in the value clarification exercise.**
2. **Help participants to develop or review an understanding of the anthropological norms listed in the social and scientific context. Do so prior to assigning the value clarification activity if you believe students will have difficulty understanding and using these procedural values.**
3. **Locate, or have students locate, the Amazon jungle region of South America on a map.**
4. **Prepare, or ask students to prepare, a glossary of the concepts listed in the introduction.**
5. **Determine whether you will place students in small groups to discuss their individual choices in the rank-ordering exercise before engaging in large group discussion.**
6. **Modify the discussion starters, if necessary, to make the value sheet fit with what you are teaching.**

Social and Scientific Context

For purposes of this exercise you are to assume that the following conditions are true:

1. You are seriously considering the possibility of studying to be an anthropologist.
2. Due to the efforts of your uncle, John Kenner, you have been invited to join an anthropological expedition into the Amazonian jungle.
3. You accept and adhere to the viewpoint that an anthropologist should and does:
   a. Systematically collect data about the behavior of people.
   b. Identify how behavior clusters into patterns, with each element being important for an understanding of a given pattern.
   c. Determine and explain the functions served by different elements and patterns of behavior.
   d. Be objective, never allowing biases and values to color observations.
   e. Avoid engaging in actions likely to alter the life style and culture of the people being studied.
4. You know what an anthropologist means when he uses such terms as structure, function, norm, folkway, mores, taboo, institution, role, and status.

The expeditionary force that you join is searching for an obscure Indian tribe, the Oktu. Except for isolated and brief accidental encounters, members of this tribe have never had contact with people from the technological cultures of the modern world. Only a few fragments of information relating to members of the tribe have been reported. The principal reason for the scarcity of knowledge about the Oktu is that members of the tribe have always chosen to run or hide when strangers happened upon them. The purpose of the anthropological expedition is to locate, observe, and describe the culture of the Oktu.

An analysis of the fragmentary data available has indicated that the Oktu have most frequently been sighted along the banks of a tributary of the Amazon River. Accordingly, the expedition moves up the Amazon and begins to penetrate the tributary stream. Three days later, the Oktu are sighted on the bank of the stream. To your surprise, and to that of other members of the anthropological team, the Oktu do not run or hide. Instead, they stand and watch as your boats are beached. For the first time in recorded history the Oktu do not flee from strangers.

Although the Indians do not flee, they do ignore the presence of your group. Efforts to communicate prove futile because the Oktu refuse to cooperate. Apparently, members of the tribe are ignoring the presence of the strange group now camped in their midst. Nevertheless, the Oktu can be observed, their behavior can be described, and their culture can be analyzed.

For twelve weeks your group of anthropologists observes the Oktu. By the thirteenth week, all are convinced that something is drastically wrong. A conference is called to discuss the situation. Your uncle, John Kenner, summarizes the reasons why members of the team believe that something is wrong.

1. All recorded instances of contact with the tribe have reported that the Oktu respond to strangers by fleeing or hiding. The fact that the Oktu rejected flight and did not hide when your expedition arrived is inconsistent with a known pattern of behavior. Such an inconsistency demands explanation.
2. Within the last two days, leaders of the Oktu have begun to make desperate attempts to communicate with members of the anthropological group. The consensus is that they are extremely anxious, perhaps frightened. This anxiety is so severe as to make efforts to communicate almost impossible despite the sudden willingness of the Oktu to cooperate.
3. The youngest children in the group appear to have attained or to be near the age of puberty. There are no babies or young children in the group.
4. No female member of the Oktu has become obviously pregnant during the twelve weeks that your group has been camped among the tribe.
5. No member of the expedition has observed courtship patterns among the young adults of the tribe. The strong suspicion is that the Oktu are avoiding sexual activity.

Only one conclusion can be drawn. For some powerful but unknown reason, the Oktu are no longer producing children. Because of this failure to procreate, the Oktu face extinction as a unique human group.

There is no disagreement with Kenner's conclusion. However, a heated debate ensues over how members of the expedition should react to the situation. Should team members continue to behave as anthropologists? Should members of the team use their knowledge as anthropologists in order to help the Oktu? Eventually, five possible policies emerge. Each position is supported by at least one anthropologist. Despite prolonged debate kept under control by your uncle, agreement proves to be elusive.

Finally, your uncle suggests that all members accept a vote as one way of resolving the conflict. He further proposes that each member rank order the five policies from the one he believes is best to the one that he believes is worst; that the votes be tabulated; and that the policy obtaining the most support be accepted by all members of the group. All parties to the dispute agree with this means of resolving the conflict.

In line with this decision, a ballot is prepared. Consider the five policies carefully and mark the attached ballot. As you consider the five policies, remember who you are and what your scholarly values are as they were given at the beginning of the exercise. Remember, too, who you are as a person and the kind of human being you like to believe you are. Finally, remember the particular situation toward which your vote is directed and the simple people whose fate you are helping to determine.

On the Edge of Objectivity

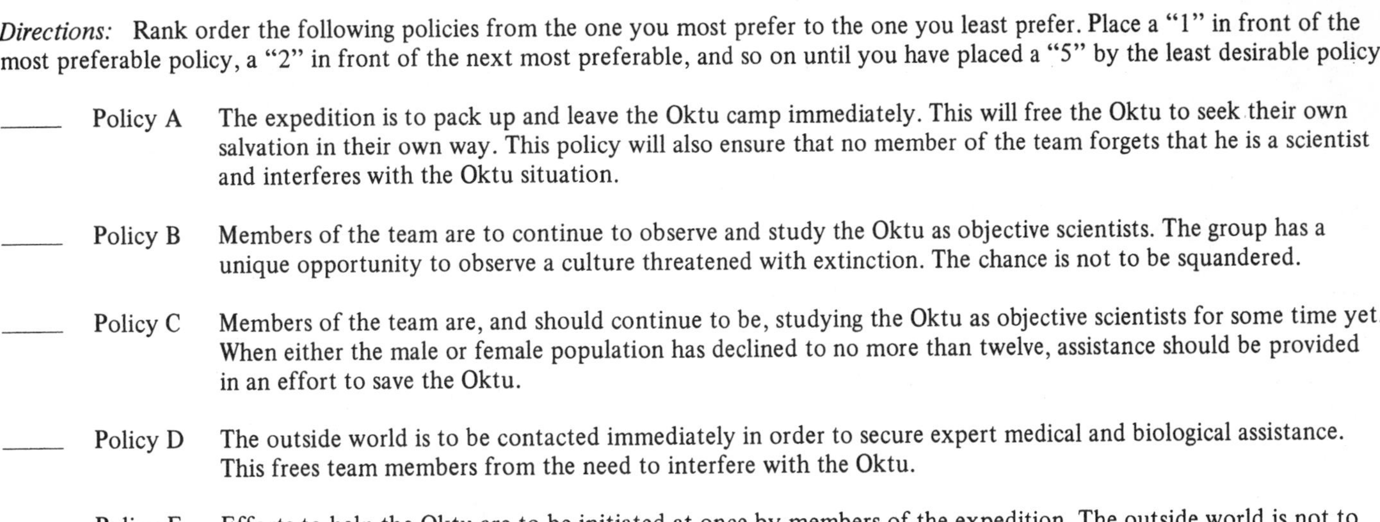

BALLOT

Directions: Rank order the following policies from the one you most prefer to the one you least prefer. Place a "1" in front of the most preferable policy, a "2" in front of the next most preferable, and so on until you have placed a "5" by the least desirable policy.

_____ Policy A The expedition is to pack up and leave the Oktu camp immediately. This will free the Oktu to seek their own salvation in their own way. This policy will also ensure that no member of the team forgets that he is a scientist and interferes with the Oktu situation.

_____ Policy B Members of the team are to continue to observe and study the Oktu as objective scientists. The group has a unique opportunity to observe a culture threatened with extinction. The chance is not to be squandered.

_____ Policy C Members of the team are, and should continue to be, studying the Oktu as objective scientists for some time yet. When either the male or female population has declined to no more than twelve, assistance should be provided in an effort to save the Oktu.

_____ Policy D The outside world is to be contacted immediately in order to secure expert medical and biological assistance. This frees team members from the need to interfere with the Oktu.

_____ Policy E Efforts to help the Oktu are to be initiated at once by members of the expedition. The outside world is not to be contacted.

Discussion Starters

1. What are some of the most important norms an anthropologist uses to guide his behavior?
2. When an anthropologist studies a culture, what does he look for?
3. What problem does the anthropological group presented here encounter?
4. Which policy did you rank as most preferable? (State it in your own words.) Suppose an anthropologist asked you to justify your position. What would you say?
5. Suppose officials of the South American country that allowed your group to seek out and observe the Oktu . asked you to justify your position. How would you respond?
6. Suppose an outstanding ethical (or religious) leader asked you to justify your position. How would you respond?
7. Which policy did you rank as least preferable? (State it in your own words.) How would you justify this ranking if asked to do so by an anthropologist? If asked by a humanist?
8. Some swords are designed to cut with both sides of the blade. Can scientific objectivity become such a sword? Explain.
9. If you supported a policy leading to interference with the Oktu society, what would be your reaction if the Oktu rejected your efforts to "save" them by fleeing deeper into the jungle?
10. Our society frequently searches for precedents to justify policies and behaviors that before were considered improper or wrong. How would you feel if the policy you supported as most preferable established a precedent in the area of cultural interference by anthropologists? By humanitarians? By revolutionaries?

26. Church, State, and Political Agent

TEACHER PREPARATION

1. **Secure sufficient copies of the value sheet for each student.**
2. **Review the First Amendment to the United States Constitution.**
3. **Modify the discussion starters to make them consistent with your purposes.**
4. **Consider creating small groups, each one a town council, and asking them to seek consensus on the rank ordering required by the value sheet.**
5. **Consider following up this activity by role-playing the situation as given, but add leaders of the church in question, who may observe and question the work of the town council as it makes its decision.**

Social and Scientific Context

Although you live in a small, rather conservative community (population of 5,000), you like to think of yourself as an open-minded, liberal sort of person. And, in fact, everyone is impressed with the way you pick up new ideas and follow current fads. Most everyone is aware that you have taken part in various civil rights and peace demonstrations and are committed to the need for reforms in various segments of American society. Last year, in a burst of community spirit, you joined several civic clubs, the volunteer fire department, the PTA, and a well-established, prominent religious group. Like most people, you haven't thought much about religion and are rather uncomfortable when it is being discussed, but if someone pinned you down, the following statements would be characteristic of your beliefs:

- All religions are based on the worship of a higher power.
- Any religion is all right as long as it doesn't interfere with someone else's right to worship as he sees fit.
- Freedom of religion is one of the great guarantees of the Constitution.
- A man with some kind of religion is better than a man with no religion at all.

One night a town meeting is called to discuss an immediate problem. The American Church of Satan has purchased an old house on the edge of the city and plans to use it as a "house of worship" and a center for teaching white magic and mystic arts. Although no one will admit it, there is an atmosphere of fear and panic.

After a lengthy discussion in which many views are expressed, several possible ways of dealing with the situation are advanced:

1. Pass a zoning ordinance, retroactive to the previous year, that would prohibit using the location of the old house for a public meeting place but that would also stop construction of a new movie theater down the block.
2. Simply tell the American Church of Satan that it is unwelcome in the community and give members a deadline for leaving, after which they will be arrested for trespassing.
3. Do nothing about the church because they have as much right as any religious group to be in town.
4. Do nothing, but ask the police to watch the house closely to make sure nothing illegal or immoral is occurring.
5. Ask the group to appear before a town meeting and to explain their beliefs and practices; then decide what to do.
6. Ask the church to deposit $10,000 in a local bank as an insurance against possible damage to the city or its inhabitants.

The mayor then asks you to prepare a leaflet in which you rank the proposals in order, from the best solution to the worst. Although you are pleased to do so, you are worried because you had planned to run for public office, and how you handle this assignment may well determine whether or not the community will support you.

In keeping with my beliefs I rank the proposal as follows:

____ *Proposal 1:* Zoning Ordinance.
____ *Proposal 2:* Ask to Leave.
____ *Proposal 3:* Leave Alone.
____ *Proposal 4:* Police Supervision.
____ *Proposal 5:* Appear at Town Meeting.
____ *Proposal 6:* Security Deposit.

I selected proposal ____ as best because ________________

____

____

I selected proposal ____ as worst because ________________

____

____

Discussion Starters

1. Describe the nature of the problem this situation requires you to resolve.
2. What is the difference between the best solution and the worst solution?
3. Assuming the situation were true, how would you feel about being the person who had to make this decision? Why?
4. Do you consider yourself to be liberal or conservative? Why? What are you according to this worksheet?
5. In view of this exercise, do you think you can say you favor freedom of religion, in the broadest sense of the phrase? Explain your answer.

27. Getting 'The Load' Off Your Mind

TEACHER PREPARATION

1. **Identified in this activity are these distinct sections:**
   a. **The social and scientific context: the news releases.**
   b. **Rank-order exercise 1, related to the news releases.**
   c. **The social and scientific context: the television broadcast.**
   d. **Rank-order exercise 2, related to the television broadcast.**
   e. **The social and scientific context: the political scene.**
   f. **Rank-order exercise 3, related to the national referendum.**
2. **For purposes of this exercise, the social and scientific situation you will ask students to respond to is contrived. There is, however, a growing body of literature suggesting that these circumstances, while fictional, are not fantasy. (You may wish to point out to students that the organizations, individuals, and events in this situation are invented.)**
3. **Determine how many of the rank-order tasks you will ask students to engage in. The third rank-order exercise, identified as the national referendum, is the focal point of this activity and is to be completed.**
4. **Secure copies of the value sheet for each student. If you intend for students to complete all three rank-order exercises, you may wish to distribute only one component at a time. (A component is a social and scientific context situation with its adjoining rank-order exercise.)**
5. **Decide whether you are going to discuss each rank-order exercise after the students have completed them or whether you will discuss all three at the same time, following the completion of all the exercises.**
6. **Identify vocabulary words likely to cause difficulty for your students and develop a glossary (on ditto or on the board).**
7. **Decide how many days you will devote to this activity. You may wish to spend some time developing a background by using articles and concepts previously studied in class or articles listed under the heading of genetics in the bibliography of the AAAS (American Association for the Advancement of Science).**
8. **Decide whether you want students to rank order the "national referendum" exercise individually or as members of a group seeking consensus. If you decide to make it an individual matter, consider having students vote anonymously (using secret ballots) and using a committee to compile and report results before or after discussion of the value sheet.**
9. **Consider varying the presentation by allowing two panels of students to present and elaborate on the conclusions and recommendations of the television broadcast by the panel of scholars—much like news commentators and analysts follow other national broadcasts.**

Social and Scientific Context: The News Releases

The following news items have appeared in the daily newspapers that are typically read in all sections of the nation and have been the subject of radio and television news programs and newscasts. All have come to your attention within the last twelve months.

News Release 1

The National Health Commission (NHC) has issued a bulletin reporting an alarming increase in persons born with mental or physical defects. The bulletin, as issued, contains data showing substantial increases within the last fifty years in the incidence of diseases that can either be associated with or are known to be transmitted by heredity. Of these cases of inherited diseases and disabilities, the most common are hemophilia, Huntington's chorea, phenylketonuria, sickle cell anemia, and mongolism.

News Release 2

At a noontime news conference, the National Commissioner of the Federal Law Enforcement Agency (FLEA) summarized a report compiled over a two-year period by the Presidential Commission on Criminal Behavior. According to the commissioner, the nation must now accept and confront the facts about crime.

"Fact number 1: For a number of decades the number of serious crimes committed against persons has exhibited a dramatic tendency to increase. After dark, the major cities of America are jungles that fewer and fewer citizens are willing to enter unarmed.

"Fact number 2: The Presidential commission has identified and described certain categories of persons to whom the spiraling growth of crimes committed against persons can be attributed. Quite often, the potential criminal can be identified; however, law enforcement officers cannot act until they have evidence that a crime has been planned, attempted, or committed. And for the victim, this is often too late.

"Fact number 3: A number of categories of persons likely to commit serious crimes are in families whose histories are filled with criminals.

"Fact number 4: As the population increases, law enforcement officers must realistically expect the current rate of serious crimes against persons to continue and perhaps to increase slightly."

The commissioner states that he is limiting himself at this time to a presentation of the factual conclusions that can be derived from the work of the commission. Asked if he anticipated any controversy when the recommendations of the commission are published (in about three months according to one knowledgeable source), the commissioner acknowledged that this might be the case but did not consider it appropriate to comment further until the President has had time to analyze and evaluate policy implications of the commission's conclusions.

News Release 3

In a brief statement distributed without comment today, the National Commission on Education Measurement (NCEM) reported findings based on the administration of an intelligence test to a sample of elementary- and secondary-school students. According to the statement, an analysis of test results indicates that the number of children with scores characteristic of mentally defective children has exceeded expected percentages by approximately 4 percent.

The statement, handed to reporters by the National Director of Testing, who refused to answer questions, stated that efforts to correlate these findings with environmental factors had not been fruitful. The statement concluded with the unelaborated comment that "some other factor, possibly hereditary, could explain the results of the survey."

News Release 4

The Board of Directors of the National Association for Mental Health has announced a major change in its policy for awarding research grants to scholars and research institutes. The NAMH, reported to control funds in excess of $15 billion, has in the past exercised considerable influence on universities and scholars through its power to fund research.

At a noon news conference, the Executive Secretary of the NAMH reported that no further research projects will be granted NAMH moneys unless they are directed at either defining the social implications of genetic research or designing social policies capable of helping man cope with possibilities present in his increasing store of genetic-related knowledge.

Quizzed as to the basis for this decision, the executive secretary made a brief statement:

"The number of seriously mentally ill has increased at a rate three times that of population growth. The greatest increase has occurred in segments of our society now known to have had a long history of such illnesses. Despite major public and private efforts to control the conditions believed to foster such illnesses, their numbers have continued to increase with little prospect of change. A crisis is looming—a crisis in which knowledge of genetics as a factor in social policy will be critical. In order to address itself to this emergency, the board of directors of the NAMH felt that they had no choice but to focus all available resources on the field of genetics in regard to its social implications."

News Release 5

The Department of Welfare (DOW) released its annual progress report today. The report revealed that the department now spends more money than any other federal agency, with the sole exception of the Department of Defense. Reading from a prepared statement, the department's press secretary stated:

"The number of welfare recipients continues to increase with incredible speed, while the living standard of those so assisted declines with discouraging regularity.

"The major reason for the lack of progress in this area is associated with the fact that a large number of families have remained on welfare rolls for generations without improving their living standards or significantly reducing the size of their families.

"For the forseeable future, the budget of the Department of Welfare will continue to become larger. This will be necessary if we are to maintain the status quo."

Rank-Order Exercise 1: The News Releases (optional)

The news reports identified here relate to a number of personal and social problems in contemporary America. Suppose you could take steps to correct a number of these problems as listed below. Suppose further that you could only deal with one problem at a time. You would then need to solve the most important problem first, then the second, then the third, then the fourth, and finally the fifth. Show the order in which you would attack the problems listed here by marking the one you would work on first with a "1," the one you would focus on second with a "2," and so forth, until you have rank ordered all five problems.

_____ The increase in crimes against persons in large cities.

_____ Physical deformities due to genetic defects.

_____ Growth of welfare rolls without substantial personal and social improvement for recipients of funds.

_____ Diseases that can be attributed to hereditary causes.

_____ The need to know more about the social implications and possibilities of new breakthroughs in science and, in this instance, of genetic knowledge.

Social and Scientific Context: The Television Broadcast

Aspects of the current scene such as those identified in the news releases have bothered you as you have become aware of them. However, you have never bothered to think about them as a group of related information. You become intrigued about the relationships between these reports when you happen to see the television program guide describing an upcoming special. You decide to watch a two-hour prime time television program on the subject of "Genetics and the Future of the Human Race," organized and presented by a group of well-known scholars from many fields. The program is sponsored by one of the major foundations, noted for its reputable and high-quality productions.

As you watch, you learn that these scholars (from such fields as science, philosophy, the arts, education, theology, medicine, social science, and psychology) have been meeting with one another for over five years. You learn that they have done extensive research and reading in the areas related to human heredity and genetic loading. You learn that they have set up several corresponding committees to share and examine their thoughts and feelings. As a result of their association and work, these scholars have become convinced that the United States is facing a major social catastrophe. Furthermore, they have predicted some conclusions and likely outcomes warranted by the overwhelming empirical evidence and have agreed on a list of policies necessary for the preservation of our nation and its culture.

For the first hour the panel presents supporting data and evidence and identifies and elaborates on five conclusions that must be drawn from the data. These conclusions are:

1. Although mankind has increased his life span and has kept alive individuals who would have died were it not for advances in medical knowledge and technology, man has not improved his species. He has instead endangered it. Persons possessing inferior survival qualities due to genetic inheritance have not died. They are being kept alive and are transmitting these inferior traits to others. The "genetic pool" of the human species, instead of becoming stronger through the operation of principles of natural selection, is, in reality, becoming polluted with inferior, weakening genetic qualities.
2. As our "genetic pool" continues to weaken, a greater number of persons in our population will become victims and transmitters of hereditary defects. The end product will be a gradual increase in the number of all hereditary diseases, defects, and deformities.
3. The nonselective use of medical advances to help potential polluters of the genetic pool to remain alive will further weaken the genetic resources of man. This will result in a downhill spiral of the human species.
4. As a society, we can determine that we will use scientific knowledge to protect the human species. Enough knowledge of genetics and heredity exists for man to develop rational policies as to how such knowledge will be used and to protect man from its irresponsible use. Current genetic knowledge can be coupled with the technical skills and equipment of the medical profession for our society to make substantial gains in population control through genetic selectivity.

5. Man is much better equipped with knowledge of genetics, heredity, and selective population control than he is with rules and procedures for developing and implementing ethical and moral policies for using such knowledge to improve himself individually and socially. The group feels a moral and social obligation to present its recommendations to the public in order to initiate discussion among and action by groups of concerned Americans. The results, it is hoped, will be the enactment of laws by the legislatures, the interpretation of the laws by the courts, and the enforcement of the laws by the executive departments of various levels of government designed to prevent a national disaster.

During the second hour of their presentation, panel members recommend the following policies, very deliberately considering the social consequences of each policy in terms of scientific, social science, humanistic, educational, religious, and philosophical implications. The policies so recommended by the members of the learned panel are:

1. Require all citizens to undergo a standard genetic analysis profile to determine the extent to which they carry defective genes.
2. Sterilize immediately all individuals who possess mental or physical abnormalities associated with genetic defects and, in the future, destroy such persons at birth.
3. Sterilize all persons capable of transmitting defective genes to an offspring.
4. Sterilize all persons born into families with long histories of criminality, unemployment, vagrancy, poverty, or mental illness.
5. Sterilize all children who score less than 70 on a standard intelligence test at the time they attain puberty.
6. Enact these policies into national law without delay and create a Bureau of Genetics to administer and to enforce these policies rigorously.
7. Develop new and relevant codes of ethics related to the use of social and scientific knowledge.

With the last policy recommended, the panel leader apologized for burdening lay citizens with such weighty concerns and prayed that they would think, decide, and act before it was too late.

Rank-Order Exercise 2: The Television Broadcast (optional)

All of us assign more importance to some people than we do to others. Those important to us are likely to influence the way we behave and to be significant to us as agents who help us to appraise our performance as human beings. On the other hand, when these people violate our expectations, we are frequently upset and sometimes outraged. Below you will find a number of persons who were represented on the panel. Mark the person you would be most outraged (or surprised) to find making these recommendations with a "1," the person who next most outrages (or surprises) you with a "2," and so forth, until you have ranked all the persons listed.

_____ A family doctor.
_____ A religious leader (minister, priest, rabbi).
_____ A political leader known for his humanitarianism.
_____ A scientist.
_____ A social worker.
_____ A psychiatrist.

Social and Scientific Context: The Political Scene

Your reaction to the televison broadcast is mixed. You are glad these people chose to speak and yet you wish they had not. You are moved to support the policies they recommend but at the same time feel compelled to reject the policies. You are not alone. Americans ally themselves into groups, some supporting and some rejecting the conclusions and recommendations of the panel; some accepting the conclusions but rejecting what they call the unwarranted radicalism of the recommendations; some supporting acceptance of some of the recommendations after calmly considering all the alternatives, both those offered as well as those not offered by the panel; and some wanting to implement all the policies immediately, without any change whatsoever. In effect, Americans polarize themselves into groups favorably disposed toward panel recommendations and groups strongly opposed to the recommendations. Your friends belong to both camps, and each side seeks to persuade you. Their efforts become more insistent during preconvention presidential primaries in which two candidates compete to win the nomination of your political party in order to run against the man who has occupied the White House for the last four years. It is during the course of this competition that you begin to sort your ideas and values about this subject.

Two men vie for the nomination of your party. The favorite candidate senses an issue and a program that would vault him not only into the presidential nomination of his party but into the White House as well. In general, he speaks of the commitment, the concern, the scholarship, and the responsibility with which the panel has acted. Although he stops short of accepting all the recommendations, he does commend all the policies as being worthy of careful consideration.

A second man who is seeking the nomination of your party, but who is given little chance of obtaining many primary election or convention votes, also senses that the panel has presented him with an issue he can employ.

"If elected," he tells his small audiences, "I will take immediate and effective steps to limit further research in the field of genetics. I will classify as 'top secret' all genetic knowledge now available that contains potentially damaging consequences for our people. All those who advocate the cold scientific use of genetic knowledge and fail to have human compassion will find themselves facing an implacable enemy who will take steps to make certain that those who preach their creed are not supported directly or indirectly by federal moneys."

In response, the favorite candidate speaks of the social irresponsibility and irrational behavior of his opponent. And he publicly affirms, in large part, the work of the panel that presented the broadcast.

When the dust has settled from the major primaries, the favorite has won all of them. However, whereas he had been expected to win the votes of 60 to 65 percent of the party faithful, his greatest margin was 53 percent of the vote; and in two states, his challenger has surprised everyone by carrying more than 49 percent of the vote. In effect, had the dark horse candidate secured an increase of less than 1 percent in these two states, he would have entered the nominating convention with a good chance of winning the nomination of his party. Consequently, the favorite's stand on the recommendations presented by the panel has almost cost him a nomination that he appeared to have wrapped up prior to the television broadcast.

Getting 'The Load' Off Your Mind

While the two aspirants for the nomination of your party were forced to react immediately to the television broadcast, the man who already occupies the White House and whose nomination is assured, has had time to gauge the winds of public opinion. Observing the success that the unsuccessful candidate has had with the issue, the President has built his re-election campaign on the pledge that "The people will decide. The general will will be done." He has proposed that if elected, and if given the support of majorities in both the House and the Senate, he will conduct a national referendum to "let the people decide." The plain citizen, Mr. Average American, "in which the wisdom of the nation has always been cherished and protected," would be allowed to determine the direction of the policies involving the use of genetic knowledge. "I will go to the people, and the people will be heard" the President announces when he accepts the formal nomination of his party. His opponent, having committed himself during the primaries, has no room in which to maneuver, for he has already endorsed the recommendations of the panel of scholars.

Not surprising, then, the President wins his bid for reelection and carries majorities from his party into both the House and the Senate. True to his campaign pledge, the President appoints a blue-ribbon committee to draw up possible policies concerning the search for and use of genetic knowledge, especially as it relates to the problem of "genetic loading." The committee is to examine relevant data and to consider every possible alternative in compiling its recommendations. The President has told the nation that these recommendations will be presented to the people for their consideration within ninety days of the completion of the committee's work. The people will then be allowed to make their will known to the Congress and to the world.

Having completed their work, the committee hands its recommendations to the President. It is now time for the national referendum.

Rank-Order Exercise 3: The National Referendum

At this time, you are about to cast your vote in the national referendum. You are not given an option of expressing your feelings and preferences toward the original policies suggested by the panel of scholars. Instead, you must rank order a number of possible public policies identified and compiled by the committee appointed by the President. When you have finished studying the background leading up to this vote, secure a ballot and rank order the choices from best to worst.

BALLOT

National Referendum to Determine the General Will With Regard to Genetic Knowledge—in Accordance With Commitments of the President and Laws Enacted by Congress.

Rank order the following policies from the one you most prefer to the one that you least prefer, using the numbers 1 through 10 to designate your opinions.

_____ Destroy all existing evidence, equipment, theoretical papers, and other published materials associated with the social application of genetic knowledge.

_____ Monitor the activity of scientists engaged in genetic-related research and censor all monographs and books that such scientists seek to publish or publicize at national meetings.

_____ Cut off all funds and support-mechanisms for research, development, and dissemination of genetic knowledge. Pursuant to this goal, withdraw the tax-exemption privileges of private foundations funding such work.

_____ Allocate no new federal funds to help in genetic research.

_____ Confine or deport scientific and social leaders who continue to support and advocate genetic policies using television channels that belong to the people.

_____ Request the resignation of all governmental scientists and departmental officials who have advocated the exploration or design of policies based on genetic knowledge.

_____ Marshal a force of agents, trained in the skills of technicians, to seek employment with and report the activities of scholars and scientists associated with or suspected of being inclined to support policies based on a concern with genetic loading.

_____ Collect all scientific equipment purchased by individuals pursuing this line of research as part of a research grant funded by the government. This includes hardware (instruments) and software (reports and books) that have been developed using federal money and that, in truth, belong to the people.

_____ Identify scientists known to support genetic-oriented policies. Inform broadcast stations (radio and television) that providing favorable coverage to these scientists or to their work is at the risk of their FCC license.

_____ Provide funds for the development of instructional materials for use in elementary-school, junior-high, and high-school classes. Such materials will stress the evil consequences present in genetic research and the application of genetic knowledge. Require no less than two six-week units between grades seven and twelve for a student to obtain a high-school diploma.

Discussion Starters

1. In your own words, briefly describe the situation presented in this episode as you experienced it. What circumstances did you have to deal with? What feelings were aroused? What actions did you want to take?
2. In terms of the situation presented here, how can scientific knowledge and inferences drastically affect personal, social, and political behavior?
3. When the scientist begins to explore ways of applying his knowledge in order to influence personal, social, and political behavior, he must risk controversy. How would you explain this facet of the work of the scientist?
4. How can personal, social, and political decisions influence the work of the scientist?
5. Should man be concerned with genetic loading? List consequences that support your position.
6. Suppose you wanted to justify man engineering his development as a species—how would you state your grounds?
7. How might genetic knowledge be used to support a policy of national genocide?
8. Develop the outlines of an ethical code of conduct for scientists interested in genetic engineering that would make you feel secure.

9. Frame your own set of policies (make this the list that you would have preferred to find in the national referendum). How does your set differ from those offered by the panel? From those you found on the ballot?

28. On Being an Important Person

TEACHER PREPARATION

1. **Secure sufficient copies of the social and scientific context for each student to have a copy.**
2. **Make certain the social and scientific context is understood before proceeding to the rank-order task.**
3. **Determine how you will help students relate this context to the unit of work they are studying; generate questions likely to elicit statements of relationship from students.**
4. **Explain carefully what the term "rank order" means.**

Social and Scientific Context

The time is the first decade of the twentieth century. The "progressive" spirit is sweeping the United States. For purposes of this exercise, you are to assume you are living during this period of time. Every town meeting, religious gathering, and casual conversation you participate in eventually results in discussions of needed reforms in America. Everyone seems to believe that he is an authority on what is happening and what needs to be done. Everyone claims to know what and how progressives think, believe, and feel.

You are an adherent of the progressive philosophy. Because of your commitment to the necessity for reforms within certain sections of American society, you have become an activist in the movement. Your association with progressives in your state has helped you to identify the major characteristics of the progressive movement as they relate to your activities. The following statements are characteristic of your beliefs and practices:

1. The federal government should regulate and limit trusts and monopolies.
2. Municipal governments must be cleaned up and reformed.
3. Equal rights for women, especially in the area of the franchise, must be granted.
4. Expansion abroad should increase at a more rapid pace to strengthen the nation against the traditionally powerful European countries.
5. Laws to support and protect the working man must be written, legislated, and administered.
6. Social justice for all groups of Americans must be guaranteed.
7. A continuous redistribution of wealth should occur (such as through an income tax or graduated inheritance tax).

Several pieces of legislation have been proposed for passage by Congress. Here is a brief description of these items:

Bill Number 1: *The Reclamation Bill*
If enacted, funds received from the sale of public lands are to be reserved. The President is empowered to retain public lands for public use. This measure is expected to initiate a systematic government program for the establishment of public parks.

Bill Number 2: *The Elkins Bill*
If enacted, railroads will be prohibited from arbitrarily setting rates for shipping products from one destination to another. This bill also prohibits the payment or acceptance of rebates for such shipments. It would include stiff punishments for all violators convicted of breaking the law.

Bill Number 3: *The Pure Food and Drug Bill*
If enacted, a printed statement will be required on all packaged food and drug items describing the ingredients and contents of the package. All sales or attempted sales of adulterated food and drug items will be prohibited. A *meat inspection amendment* has been added to this bill and would require government grading and inspection of all meat products.

Bill Number 4: *The Immigration Bill*
If enacted, this bill will amend an earlier immigration act to exclude paupers, criminals, anarchists, and diseased persons from entry into the United States.

Bill Number 5: *The Income Tax Bill*
If enacted, Congress will be authorized to tax the income of individuals from all sources without regard to census and without apportionment among the states. Should enough states ratify this bill, it will become an amendment to the U.S. Constitution.

Bill Number 6: *The Mann Bill*
If enacted, it will become a federal crime to transport women across the state lines for illegal and immoral purposes.

As a participant in the progressive movement, you are vitally interested in each of these proposed laws. You are especially interested in new bills brought before Congress because a number of your friends respect your judgments and opinions about pending legislation and some are personally acquainted with members of the local and state Congressional delegation. Many have even written letters to their Congressmen about certain issues after discussing them with you. Your knowledge and opinions have gained you such a reputation that the editor of the local newspaper, upon hearing of the six new bills being considered by Congress, asks you to help him write an editorial for the Sunday edition of the newspaper.

The newspaper is subscribed to by over 90 percent of the households in your town. It is highly regarded in the community and its sound reputation has made it quite influential. Prior to beginning work on an editorial, the editor asks you to prepare by completing three tasks:

1. In your own words, state what you believe as a progressive.
2. Rank order the proposed six bills in order from the bill that would accomplish the most good to the one that would accomplish the least good.
3. State specifically the basis upon which you selected the best and worst bill when you rank ordered them.

You suddenly realize that this editorial is a trial balloon to determine the general public's attitudes toward progressivism. You are reminded by friends and acquaintances that, while progressivism is a popular subject of conversation in the community, progressives are looked upon with suspicion and distrust. They have often been labeled as "do-gooders" and subversives by business and financial interests in the town. Although you have the opportunity to inform the public as to the beneficial aspects of the movement, you are aware that should your efforts fail to convince the public, the progressive movement in your town will be harmed.

You decide to work carefully, to state clearly your commitments, and to use these to rank order the six bills rationally. Forms to assist you in fulfilling the three tasks assigned by the editor are provided on the following pages.

On Being an Important Person

TASK 1 WORKSHEET

In my own words, I as a progressive believe:

1. ____________________

2. ____________________

3. ____________________

4. ____________________

5. ____________________

6. ____________________

7. ____________________

After completing this summary, you may wish to refer back to the list at the beginning of this value sheet.

On Being an Important Person

TASK 2 WORKSHEET

In the space provided to the left of the items below, rank order the six proposed bills, from the one you believe to be the most needed (number 1) to the least needed (number 6).

_____ Bill Number 1: The Reclamation Bill.

_____ Bill Number 2: The Elkins Bill.

_____ Bill Number 3: The Pure Food and Drug Bill.

_____ Bill Number 4: The Immigration Bill.

_____ Bill Number 5: The Income Tax Bill.

_____ Bill Number 6: The Mann Bill.

TASK 3 WORKSHEET

I selected the ______________________________ Bill as best. My basis for this

preference is: ______________________________

____

____

____

I selected the ______________________________ Bill as worst. My basis for this

preference is: ______________________________

____

____

____

On Being an Important Person

Discussion Starters

1. What is the main difference between the grounds you cited for legislation most needed and that least needed?
2. Is the basis for your first choice for needed legislation congruent with a modern-day progressivism?
3. Devise a set of beliefs one would hold if he considered himself a modern progressive.
4. Are there persons alive today that you consider to be progressive? Who are they?
5. How do you feel toward the beliefs used to describe a progressive?
6. What type of legislation do you think a person characterized as a progressive would support today? Would be opposed to today?
7. What type of balance should one maintain between his individual freedom and social responsibility?
8. Do you consider yourself to be a progressive?
9. Assume that the situation is true. What are the effects of being an important person? To what degree are these consequences consistent with your experiences?

29. Justice In a Pinch

TEACHER PREPARATION

1. **Secure sufficient copies of the value sheet for each student.**
2. **Decide whether you wish students to work individually or in small groups as they rank order the possible courses of action. If you use small groups, decide further whether students will be allowed to resolve differences of opinion by vote, or whether they must find a basis for consensus when disagreements occur.**
3. **Adjust the discussion starters in order to make this activity a part of the unit you are teaching.**

Social and Scientific Context

At one point or another, all of us have had to decide whether or not we were justified in "breaking" a rule or "bending" the law. Imagine that you have an opportunity to help determine what should occur in the following situation.

> Ocala, Florida–Police here report they have apprehended two men who allegedly chased a calf down a back country road and ran it down with their car.
>
> Officers said that Bob Smith, 52, and his brother-in-law, James Jens, 34, were arrested as they prepared to butcher the calf on a table in Smith's garage.
>
> Smith, an unemployed father of eight, said, "I knew what I done wrong but I can't afford to buy meat at these prices, and my family's got to eat."
>
> Smith and Jens were arrested and placed in jail.

A controversy erupts as to what should happen to Smith and Jens. Different persons in the community believe that different actions should be taken in order to serve the cause of justice. Seven possible actions are listed below.

Suppose you are helping to decide what will happen to Smith and Jens. Rank order the possible policies from the one that you believe is best for this situation to the one that you believe is worst for it. To do so, place a "1" by the most preferable action, a "2" by the second most preferable action, and so on until you have placed a "7" by the least preferable action.

_____ Smith and Jens should be ticketed for wreckless driving and charged with killing a fur-bearing animal without a license.

_____ Smith and Jens should be ordered to pay the owner of the calf the market value of the animal.

_____ Smith and Jens should be sent to prison.

_____ Smith and Jens should not be punished because the high cost of beef prompted their action.

_____ The court should dismiss the case since Smith and Jens aren't "real" criminals like murders, rapists, and thieves.

_____ Smith should be congratulated for trying to provide for the needs of his family.

_____ Smith and Jens should be punished, but the judge should take into consideration that Smith is unemployed and has a family.

Discussion Starters

1. What did Smith and Jens do to get into trouble?
2. What were they doing when they were caught?
3. To what degree can one consider Smith to be a man of high morals who respects the law? Explain your answer.
4. Thomas Jefferson believed that a little rebellion now and then is a good thing. How do you feel about this statement?
5. Under what circumstances would you bend the law?
6. How should Smith have fed his family?
7. Given your rank ordering of the possible actions that might be taken, what does the word justice mean to you?

30. A Mental Case, or Two

TEACHER PREPARATION

1. **Make sure that each student has copies of the two rank-order exercises in this activity.**
2. **Decide whether the background information leading up to the two exercises is to be read and described to the class or whether individual copies of this information are to be made available to each student.**
3. **Decide whether you want students to form small groups and attempt to reach a consensus after they have rank ordered the alternatives individually.**
4. **Consider inviting a member of your local mental health association to your class after this activity to help answer questions raised during the course of this activity.**
5. **Prepare a list of discussion starters consistent with your objectives.**

Social and Scientific Context

Reading is a relatively small town located in the foothills of the Appalachian Mountains. The community once had a booming economy. However, it has never recovered from the decision of a large manufacturing plant to relocate rather than to meet local environmental standards. The Reading Chamber of Commerce and the city fathers are busily engaged in efforts to attract new industries and to halt the migration of young people to other cities and towns where opportunity is greater.

Approximately six months ago, many of Reading's problems with unemployment and with a slack economy appeared to be resolved. The regional medical association applied to a large foundation for some $8 million to build and staff a large mental hospital and institution. Prior to making the application, the medical association received assurances from community and government leaders that the city of Reading would provide approximately 200 acres of land located in an unused section and designated as an industrial park. However, when the foundation agreed to grant the necessary funds and the regional medical association asked that the land be deeded to them, the city council refused to act.

Members of the council refused to act because the proposed medical facility aroused opposition almost immediately. Opponents of the mental hospital saw few advantages in the literature describing the proposed institution. Reaction to this group's stand led to the formation of a second group—one that wanted to see the mental institution established in Reading. For more than a month the city council procrastinated, and when members did act they did so by washing their hands of responsibility for the final decision. They decided that a referendum was to be held in which each citizen would exercise a vote in determining whether or not the land was to be made available for building a regional mental institution.

Three weeks prior to the referendum, those supporting the location of the mental institution in Reading hired a private polling expert to measure public opinion. He, in turn, sampled public opinion and obtained the following results:

- I believe the mental institution should be built 41%
- I believe the mental institution should not be built ... 38%
- I do not intend to vote in the referendum 6%
- I am still making my decision 10%
- I prefer to keep my opinion to myself 5%

It appears that 10 percent of the voters will make the final decision as to whether or not the mental hospital is located in Reading.

At this point, the regional medical association decides to hire a public relations consultant to help sell its case to the voters. You are selected for this task.

You have hardly arrived in Reading and begun to organize your staff and program when a local weekly publishes the following information about you, all of which is true:

1. You once suffered a mental breakdown and spent six weeks in a mental institution located in the Midwest.
2. You continue to participate in the activities of a mental health clinic and have disclosed to your friends that you believe the time spent in such participation is very worthwhile for purpose of maintaining your mental balance.
3. You have stated publicly that you would take any action, and say whatever is necessary, anytime it would be of assistance to those seeking support for mental health work.

You realize your credibility has been damaged. Nevertheless, you decide to continue the job you started, inasmuch as there would not be time for another public relations consultant to be of assistance.

You and your staff determine that your best opportunities for success require that you stress the erroneous nature of the arguments used by those that oppose the hospital and that you stress the best arguments of those who favor locating the institution in Reading. In line with these decisions, your staff develops two lists for your use. The first list contains the major arguments that have been used by those opposed to the hospital. The second list contains the major arguments that can be used in support of locating the mental institution in Reading.

Your first decision is to rank order the arguments used by opponents of the mental hospital. You do this by placing a "1" by the argument you most prefer to refute, a "2" by the argument you next prefer to refute, and so on until you have placed a "10" by the argument you least prefer to refute. The arguments are:

_____ Mental illness is contagious.

_____ Mental patients are likely to be dangerous.

_____ Elderly persons who live near mental institutions are frequently placed in mental institutions without good cause.

_____ If the mental hospital is located in Reading, the town will become a haven for misfits and will lose its attractiveness as a community in which to live.

_____ A large proportion of the inmates of the institution are likely to be there due to syphilis, with the risk that this affliction will spread.

_____ Since mental illness tends to be incurable, the institution will soon be filled and will not be available for the use of local townspeople.

_____ New workers and personnel numbering close to 2,000 may introduce irresponsible or dangerous voices in the community.

_____ Many of the inmates will be homosexuals and social deviants.

_____ Mentally questionable youth will be introduced into the community. When these young people intermarry with the youth of Reading, mentally defective children are likely to weaken the human stock of Reading.

Next, you rank order the arguments you believe are likely to convince uncommitted voters to vote to give the regional medical association the land it needs in order to build the mental institution. You place a "1" by the argument you believe is best, a "2"

A Mental Case, or Two

A Mental Case, or Two

by the argument you believe is second best, and so on until you have ranked each argument.

_____ Most persons in Reading have, at one time or another, suffered from mental illness.

_____ Mental illness is not contagious.

_____ Less than 1 percent of mental patients are considered dangerous, and of those, most are dangerous only to themselves—not to others.

_____ Mental patients are most often typical human beings.

_____ The institution will immediately give new life to the construction industry in Reading and will relieve a bad slump in real estate values.

_____ Eventually, more than 2,000 persons will be employed by the mental institution.

_____ The administrative, medical, and psychiatric staffs will introduce new and highly educated individuals into the life of the community.

_____ Due to limited space, only the most serious cases would be admitted as full-time patients in the institution.

_____ Unless Reading grants this land, it will be difficult for the city to obtain future funds from private foundations.

Discussion Starters

1. Describe the community of Reading.
2. Why did the city council decide to hold a referendum to decide the fate of the mental institution?
3. What effects did the poll have on the thinking of the people living in Reading?
4. What was your role in this exercise?
5. What is the relationship between mental health and mental illness?
6. How has literature treated the mentally ill? Cite examples to support your answer.
7. Suppose the arguments used by the opposition groups were the result of stereotyped thinking. In what ways would it be accurate to say that stereotypes are more often wrong than right? Explain.
8. Suppose the mental institution were to be built in your home town. What would your feelings be then?

PROTOCOLS

The rank-order format of the value sheet may be thought of as containing four interrelated but clearly identifiable elements:

1. A situation relevant to the unit of instruction and from which one can abstract a list of choices.
2. A list of homogeneous alternatives, usually five to twelve in number.
3. A set of clear and specific instructions to students enabling them to complete the rank-order task.
4. A set of questions or discussion starters.

The teacher may view the four components of the rank-order format as less complex than some of the earlier formats. It may well be that many teachers can develop value sheets in this format with greater ease than they can write value sheets in the formats previously discussed. Although this may be true for the teacher, the task of completing rank-order tasks requires complex responses from students. Furthermore, the follow-up discussions of this value sheet format frequently take much longer than do those formats previously presented. This is especially true if one uses the rank-order task in conjunction with small groups who are assigned the further task of seeking consensus ratings.

To design and develop value clarification activities consistent with the rank-order format, the teacher should

1. Clearly state the topic, idea, or theme he is teaching and to which the value sheet must be related.
2. Identify, locate, or contrive a situation relevant to the unit of instruction that can provide a frame of reference for the rank-order task.
3. Rewrite the situation if necessary, in order to stress the context within which students are to engage in value clarification.
4. Identify the focus of the rank-order task to be used in this particular activity (is it to focus on possible policies, consequences, or preferences?).
5. Develop a list of five to twelve homogeneous options. He must check to see if they are nearly equal in attractiveness or unattractiveness.
6. Check to see if the rank-order task is reasonable, given the situation presented in the context.
7. Check to see if the items to be rank ordered have been properly introduced with a clear and specific set of instructions.
8. Determine whether students are to share their responses in small groups. (If so, the teacher must determine the directions he or she will need to give to group members.)
9. Prepare a list of discussion starters consistent with the comprehension, relational, and valuation phases of value clarification.
10. Consider how the transition will be made from this activity in the instructional unit to the next activity planned.

Teachers following these procedures should be able to create and develop value sheets in the rank-order format that they can incorporate into their own instructional units. With this knowledge, they can select and adapt value sheets already available to them in order to meet the needs of their students and, at the same time, to make value clarification an integrated component of teaching and learning.

APTER SEVEN

HE CLASSIFICATION ORMAT OF HE VALUE SHEET

:lassification format stresses the generalization of values s particular instances. Its basic function is to indicate that iduals must often surrender desirable options in order to n others they value more highly. This format can also be to demonstrate that individuals must often accept certain in a situation in order to avoid greater ones.

ie classification format contains four elements. There is social and scientific context in which an individual (or) confronts the need to select highly valued options at xpense of other options he also values; (2) a list of nine ore options that may take the form of policy statements rom which a student must identify the three that he prefers and another three that he least prefers; (3) at two decision sheets on which students record those ns they most prefer and those options they least prefer dentify the consequences likely to result from their deci- ; and (4) follow-up questions suggestive of the kinds of tions that will be raised during discussion of the valuing de. The list of options and the decision sheets warrant er attention.

he list of options should be homogeneous. If some state- :s of consequences are used, then all statements should be essed as consequences. If some statements are expressed peratives, then all statements should be phrased as impera- . Furthermore, all options should be designed to evoke r positive or negative reactions from students—that is, a ent should wish that he could choose all the options or he could avoid all the options.

ecision sheets provide students with a structure within h they can complete the valuing activity. These also help students to engage in an analysis of the consequences of their choices. Students may be guided by these decision sheets to list the positive effects of their preferred options and the negative effects that would have resulted from the choices they chose to reject. It is better, however, to help students see the negative consequences in their preferred options and to consider the positive consequences lost by rejecting (or ignoring) other options.

When a student has completed the decision sheets provided for a classification episode, he has generalized that three options are best and that three are less desirable and to be rejected. He has also listed general consequences likely to follow from each of these decisions. In effect, the student has classified his values about a particular situation in terms of his beliefs and disbeliefs.

SAMPLES

A number of examples of the classification format are presented below. Although each contains the four components outlined above, the classification format can be styled in different fashions. It may incorporate rank ordering, and it may incorporate the search for criteria. The reader will want to be alert to these variations as well as to the basic elements required by the classification format as he studies the examples. In addition, the teacher may find it useful to complete decision sheets for some or all of the valuing episodes.

Ode to the Jailbird

31. Ode to the Jailbird

TEACHER PREPARATION

1. **Decide whether the situation leading up to the nine elements in this activity is to be put on paper and distributed to each student to read or whether it is to be read aloud and discussed.**
2. **Secure copies of the nine elements of the reform package, as well as copies of the two decision sheets, for each student.**
3. **Instruct students to complete the decision sheets as fully as possible.**
4. **Prepare a copy of discussion starters that are appropriate to your unit of instruction.**

Social and Scientific Context

You are the chairman of a citizen's group dedicated to the reconstruction of the prisons located in your state. Because of the money and prestige of members of your group, you have gained the support of the governor of your state and of a large majority of the members of the state legislature. Although a considerable amount of opposition has been expressed by prison officials and police officers, it is expected that in its next session, which opens tomorrow, the legislature will pass a prison-reform package, including nine specific recommendations, or elements of reform. However, the governor has just called you for a late-evening conference about the prison-reform legislation.

The governor informs you that he remains committed to the goals of your group but that, in studying and preparing the state budget for the next two years, he finds it will be impossible to fund the full prison-reform package. In order to complete his budget message, to be read in the morning during the opening ceremonies of the legislature, the governor asks that you inform him as to the three elements of reform you and your committee most prefer to see passed. He also asks that you inform him as to the three elements of reform you and your group would most prefer to abandon as immediate goals. He also suggests that if three elements of reform are abandoned for two years, it may be possible to pass them into law at a later date. He states that to insist on the inclusion of all the elements of reform will mean certain death to the entire prison-reform package, inasmuch as, for fiscal reasons, he could no longer support it. Because he must deliver his budget message in less than twenty-four hours, he asks that you make these decisions as quickly as possible—within the hour.

He recommends that you make the decisions alone and that you remain in the executive mansion as you wrestle with the problem. Political experience has taught him that, unless one consults with all the people involved in a particular situation, it is best not to consult with or risk running into any of these people. He reminds you that, as chairman of the group and leader of the movement for prison reform, you must speak and make a decision for the group. You really have no time to consult with the others but realize that you will be held responsible for your decision, whatever it may be.

Realizing that failure to make a decision would mean the loss of all that you have worked for, you study the different elements of reform and make your decision. You select three of the prison-reform elements as most preferable because you believe they will result in the most good. You also select three as least preferable because you believe that in surrendering them you will sacrifice fewer good effects than if you had surrendered others.

In effect, then, you are to select three that are to become law immediately, three that are not to become law in the near future, and three that may or may not become law within two years but that will probably become law eventually.

After carefully studying the following nine elements of the prison-reform package, you complete and submit your decision to the governor.

Element A: Improvement of Living Conditions

Improve the living conditions a prisoner encounters when he first enters the penal system. This includes, but is not limited to, the following steps:

1. Improvement of diet by purchasing high-quality food and by employing trained professional cooks and skilled cafeteria personnel.
2. Prevention of overcrowded conditions by building more cells, by using more minimum-security units, by reducing the number of overly armed security guards, and by early-release programs.
3. Installation of adequate heating and air-conditioning systems to provide reasonable comfort for prisoners.

Element B: Development of Recreational Programs

Develop, staff, and maintain a first-rate recreational program. Such a program includes, but is not limited to, the following:

1. Continuous organization and use of intramural sports.
2. Production and presentation of popular plays.
3. Organization of athletic teams to play other teams outside the prison.
4. Involvement in physical development programs in gymnastics and team sports.
5. Free art and handicraft materials so that prisoners may learn and proceed to use hobbies during their leisure time.

Element C: Improved Medical Services

Provide medical services consistent with the needs of the prison population. This includes, but is not limited to, the following:

1. Periodical physical examinations for all prisoners.
2. Psychiatric assistance for prisoners, especially in the area of maintaining sexual identity.
3. Maintenance of a health-care unit on a twenty-four-hour, seven-day-a-week basis.
4. Training of prisoners in health-related professions.
5. Correction of dental problems in order to maintain and improve appearance.
6. A program for improving the appearance of prisoners who have scars or other physical defects that might limit their ability to obtain a job or to lead a normal life outside the prison.

Element D: Improved Aesthetic Environment

Develop and implement a program designed to change the aesthetic environment of the prison. This includes, but is not limited to, the following:

1. Employment of a landscape engineer to develop green belts in the open spaces inside and outside the prison.
2. Employment of an interior decorator to break down the monotony of the prison interior with aesthetically pleasing modifications in coloring and accessories, and with future renovations.
3. Employment of a layout engineer who would function to coordinate alterations and new construction toward break-

ing down the image of the prison as a warehouse in which human beings are stored and stocked.

4. Provision of one cell, unlocked where feasible, for each prisoner.
5. Creation of a stockroom of furniture from which each prisoner could select items for his cell consistent with his tastes.
6. Development of a tape bank of recordings connected to each cell by an intercom system.

Element E: Self-Concept Development

Develop a program to build a positive self-concept for each prisoner in order that he may perceive himself as an important person. This includes, but is not limited to, the following:

1. Employment of well-educated prison personnel.
2. Training of prison personnel to be sensitive to and to respond to prisoners as human beings.
3. Maintenance of sensitivity among prison personnel by continuous assessment and retraining programs.
4. Provision of opportunities for prisoners to engage in discussions with prison officials in no-holds-barred sessions.
5. Allowing prisoners to periodically evaluate the prison staff with whom they have daily face-to-face contact.

Element F: Improvement of Counseling Services

Implement a program designed to improve the counseling services offered to prisoners. This includes, but is not limited to, the following:

1. Lowering the case load of counselors.
2. Increasing the amount of group counseling provided.
3. Requiring that each counselor periodically consult with members of the prisoner's immediate family, if the prisoner so desires.
4. Conducting periodic follow-up studies of prisoners to collect data by which counseling services can be improved.

Element G: Expansion of Visitation Privileges

Develop and initiate various programs that would serve to expand the visitation privileges of prisoners. This includes, but is not limited to, the following:

1. Allowing members of a prisoner's family to visit with him for extended two-to-three day periods in special facilities.
2. Allowing two- or three-week furloughs for prisoners to return home periodically.
3. Providing the necessary funds for the maintenance and, if need be, the creation of a stable home environment for the family of the prisoner.

Element H: Improvement of Educational Opportunities

Establish new, and modify existing, programs to improve the educational opportunities of prisoners. This includes, but is not limited to, the following:

1. Requiring that each prisoner, prior to release, secure the equivalent of a high-school diploma.
2. Scrapping busy work, such as the manufacture of license plates, except where prisoners volunteer to work in order to obtain a fair wage.
3. Converting vocational programs into academic courses that educate prisoners rather than occupy them.
4. Providing for prisoners to attend classes in local community colleges and universities in order to seek and receive higher degrees.
5. Initiation of programs whereby prisoners travel throughout the state, informing public school students of life in prisons while learning to relate to adults in roles prisoners may not have experienced.

Element I: Facilitation of Prisoner Return to Civilian Life

Make efforts to assist the prisoner in returning to life as a fully functioning person and member of his society. This includes, but is not limited to, the following:

1. Maintenance of halfway houses through which prisoners move toward full freedom.
2. Payment of a subsidy to industries willing to train, employ, and provide advancement opportunities for former prisoners.
3. Making it illegal for state agencies to purchase goods or services from businesses or industries that discriminate against persons who have been imprisoned.

Ode to the Jailbird

DECISION SHEET A

The three most preferable elements of prison reform are:	The major advantage of this element to the prisoner is:	The major advantage of this element to society is:
Element ____ : ________	________	________
Element ____ : ________	________	________
Element ____ : ________	________	________

DECISION SHEET B

The three least preferable elements of prison reform are:	The major advantage of this element lost to the prisoner is:	The major advantage of this element lost to society is:
Element ____ : ________	________	________
________	________	________
________	________	________
________	________	________
Element ____ : ________	________	________
________	________	________
________	________	________
________	________	________
Element ____ : ________	________	________
________	________	________
________	________	________
________	________	________

Ode to the Jailbird

Discussion Starters

1. Why does the governor ask for advice before writing his budget message?
2. Assume that the group interested in prison reform, the governor, and the majority of state legislators believe in all nine elements of the prison-reform package. How would they explain the causes of crime?
3. The emphasis of the prison-reform package was the prisoner, not the criminal. Setting aside the fact that the prisoner is one who lives in a prison, what are the similarities and differences between the prisoner and the criminal?
4. What would be the reasons law enforcement officials and prison officials would give in opposition to your reform package?
5. The costs of implementing the elements in the reform package are going to be high. In what sense could one argue that the cost of saving money is too expensive a price to pay?
6. Suppose you were a prisoner. How would you feel about "outsiders" who suggested the nine elements in this proposal? About those who opposed the nine elements?
7. Suppose, as a prisoner, you expected all of the reform package to be recommended by the governor. How would you feel when you heard the governor recommended only three of the nine elements in the program?

32. The 'Soul' Movement

TEACHER PREPARATION

1. **Secure sufficient copies of the value sheet for each student.**
2. **Distribute and discuss the social and scientific context before distributing the decision sheets.**
3. **Determine whether you want students to fill out the decision sheets individually or as members of small groups of four or five.**
4. **Decide the degree to which you want to become involved in item number 6 in the discussion starters.**
5. **Consider questions you can use to help students relate this valuing experience to the unit they are studying.**

Social and Scientific Context

The Negro has often been referred to by historians as the "forgotten man of the progressive era." His only gains were in literacy, even though Negro schools were far inferior to those attended by whites. The 1896 *Plessy v. Ferguson* Supreme Court decision helped to guarantee that "separate and equal" education facilities would remain at least separate. The political, economic, and social failures of Reconstruction were obvious to the black man. In many cases he was worse off than he had been under slavery. Progressives, while speaking of social reforms and social justice, often aided in the disfranchisement of the Negro for fear of splitting the white vote and producing a Negro victory at the polls. With the exception of Tennessee, every state that had been in the Confederacy removed black names from the voting rosters and polling booths through a combination of literacy tests, high poll taxes, threats of violence, and in some cases, actual acts of violence.

In August of 1908, in Springfield, Illinois, a bloody race riot occurred at the 100th anniversary celebration of Abraham Lincoln's birthday. The tragedy resulted in the formation of the National Association for the Advancement of Colored People (NAACP). This Association evolved from an earlier more radical organization called the Niagra Movement. A nationwide call for a conference to seek solutions for racial evils resulted in a meeting on Lincoln's birthday in 1909 and produced the NAACP. Those accepting the challenge to help remedy racial discrimination and "evils" and agreeing upon a plan of action were: Jane Addams, William Dean Howells, Livingston Farrand, John Dewey, W. E. B. Dubois, and Oswald Garrison Villard.

The policies adopted by the newly formed NAACP in 1909 included

- Abolition of all forced segregation practices.
- Provision of equal education for black and white children.
- Complete enfranchisement of the Negro.
- Enforcement of the Fourteenth and Fifteenth Amendments.
- Widening of industrial labor opportunities for Negroes.
- Increased police protection for Negroes in the South.
- Challenging in the courts those "grandfather clauses" included in some state constitutions.
- Crusades against lynchings and lawlessness directed at blacks.
- Developing "Negro consciousness" through magazines such as *Crisis,* edited by Dubois.

After examining the policies adopted during the 1909 meeting of the NAACP, turn to the attached decision sheets. On the first sheet, list the three policies you would have selected as deserving the highest priority had you attended the 1909 organizational meeting. On the same sheet, list the positive and beneficial consequences of these policies that would have resulted from their attainment. On the second sheet, list the three policies you would have selected as being lowest on your priority list. Then identify the benefits that would have been lost to the Negro if these goals were sacrificed.

DECISION SHEET A

The three policies that should be assigned top priority are:

1. ______

2. ______

3. ______

Comments: ______

The results of these policies that I would hope for are (try to list three results for each policy): ______

DECISION SHEET B

The three policies to be assigned the lowest priority are:

1. ______________________________

2. ______________________________

3. ______________________________

Comments: ______________________________

The probable benefits lost to the Negro by rejecting these policies (try to list three lost benefits for each policy): ______________________________

The 'Soul' Movement

Discussion Starters

1. Dubois was the only black officer of the early NAACP. How would you respond to an organization set up to help black people if it were conducted and financed mainly by whites?
2. Are there any other policies the NAACP should have pursued? Name them.
3. How would you have felt about the NAACP in 1909 had you been
   a. A progressive seeking to remedy social abuses?
   b. A poor Southern white?
   c. A poor Southern black?
   d. A white Southern politician?
   e. A woman?

   State the basis for your answers to each of the above.
4. What methods should the NAACP have used to pursue their goals? What methods should they have avoided using?
5. To what degree were the original founders of the NAACP progressive?
6. Imagine you are a member of a panel attempting to identify what should be done to improve the conditions of a group of people (such as Indians, migrant workers, or the Appalachian poor). What policies would you pursue?
7. Apparently, the progressives who formed the NAACP thought they could speak for the black man. To what extent did progressives believe they could speak for children? For working men? For women?
8. If someone attempts to speak for you, what are your feelings?
9. Who should speak for deprived groups?

MIRANDA
DEPORTATION.
INFERIOR GENETIC QUALITIES! ME?
HAVE YOU EVER SEEN A TREE?
HEY!
IT'S
HOT! CROWDED! HI-DENSITY!
JUST TALK...
STUFFY!
HAVE ANOTHER VITAMIN & TONIC, TOM
IT'S YOUR 137th Birthday
AFTER ALL...
Kitchell

33. In Pursuit of the General Welfare

TEACHER PREPARATION

1. **Secure copies of the following for each student:**
   a. **The social and scientific context.**
   b. **The group decision-making guide.**
   c. **The list of thirteen possible policies.**
   d. **The subcommittee report form.**
   e. **The consequential analysis form (optional).**
2. **Decide whether you intend to spend three or four days or wish to invest less time in this activity. If you only wish to use one or two days, modify the assignment by making subcommittee assignments more realistic for this time span. For example, distribute the social context situation to be read as homework and limit the assignment to the identification of positive and negative policies.**
3. **Decide how you will group students for this activity. Some options are:**
   a. **Divide the total class into groups of four to seven students and let each group function as a subcommittee.**
   b. **Have five students role-play the actions of a decision-making committee while the other students observe.**
   c. **Develop criteria as to how members of a decision-making group can be most effective. Have different groups of five students role-play while the other students observe and periodically provide the role-players with feedback.**
4. **Identify vocabulary words likely to cause difficulty for students, and develop a glossary (on ditto or on the board).**
5. **Make sure students understand the situation before they begin attempting to sort out the alternatives from which they are to make a decision.**
6. **Call attention to the study guide and ask students to work their way through it prior to public discussion. (Do this regardless of the grouping option you decide to use.)**

Social and Scientific Context

The time is the not-too-distant future. The place is a land near the United States with a culture and society much like the culture and society of the United States. The country is named Mirania, and objects associated with its culture are called Miranian. Because of its limited physical size, Mirania has only local government boards and a national government. All laws are made by a one-house congress called the General Assembly. Except for the differences in size and the absence of state governments, Mirania is much like the United States. A person born and educated in the United States would experience no culture shock were he to immigrate to Mirania, as Miranian values and norms are much the same as ours.

Miranian legislators are elected once every four years. The country's president serves for four years and is eligible for no more than two terms in the office. As in the United States, the judges of the Supreme Court are appointed by the president with the advice and consent of the General Assembly. Many other similarities exist between the two countries. Miranian visions of the "good life" are much the same as their American counterparts, and the two countries share many similar social and environmental problems.

The quality of life, and Miranian life styles, have made Mirania a highly desirable place to live. Demographers have warned that unchecked population growth will destroy the Miranian nation and culture. However, members of the General Assembly have been more committed to talk about the impending disaster than any action that would prevent such a catastrophe.

The General Assembly has advertised in other nations that Mirania faces a critical population problem within the next two decades. It has funded voluntary groups concerned with disseminating information about birth control. Schools are provided increased funds if they develop and teach units labeled "sex education" but whose primary emphasis is birth control information. The effects of these programs are, at best, delaying—immigration continues. Births mount, while medical research continues to keep the aged alive. The population continues to grow.

Worried about the results of this growth, many citizens are stirred to join groups interested in taking specific and immediate action. Eventually these groups unite to win control of the General Assembly and to elect a "population control" president. The public has given the national government a mandate to do something to check the population growth.

The newly elected General Assembly is committed to the identification of policies that will limit population growth. The leadership of the General Assembly believes that policies enacted into law should shock the unconcerned into becoming more alert, should immediately slow down population growth, should be relatively inexpensive over the long run, and should provide for the maintenance and improvement of the quality of life for the citizens of Mirania.

For the purposes of this exercise, you are a Miranian legislator elected to the General Assembly as a population control candidate. You received nearly 63 percent of the votes in your district.

The major committee to which you are assigned is the Population Control Committee. As a member of that committee, you are also appointed to serve on a subcommittee, the primary purposes of which are to consider the general area of the application of genetic knowledge and to recommend policies that the full committee can propose as bills to the General Assembly. The odds are strong that the recommendations of your subcommittee will be bills proposed by the Population Control Committee. The odds are even better that whatever bills the committee recommends will be enacted into law by the General Assembly and will be signed by the president.

DECISION-MAKING GUIDE

As a result of months of investigation and study, you and other members of the subcommittee have identified thirteen possible policies that your government could enact and enforce. (These policies are listed on page 110.) You have agreed as a group to present the full committee with the following:

1. A listing of the three policies that your subcommittee believes should be written as bills and should become laws immediately.
2. A listing of the three policies that your subcommittee believes are unworthy of further consideration.
3. A statement of your subcommittee's basis for recomending the three policies selected.
4. A statement of your subcommittee's reasons for believing the second three are unworthy of further consideration.
5. A third listing made up of those policies neither recommended nor rejected (optional).
6. A listing of the social and environmental consequences likely to occur if each of your recommendations becomes law. Each policy proposed should have its consequences explored individually (optional).

Before reaching a decision as a group, your subcommittee has agreed to follow three simple procedural rules:

1. Each member of the subcommittee will independently rank order all thirteen policies from the most desirable to the least desirable.
2. Disagreements between individual members of the subcommittee are to be resolved through discussion and persuasion. You cannot and will not allow a decision by simple majority vote.
3. Final decisions of the subcommittee will be summarized and signed by all members of the group to signify that the decisions are agreeable to all members of the subcommittee.

Possible Public Policies Related to Genetic Knowledge and Its Application

1. Provide monetary subsidies to parents found to possess superior genetic qualities likely to be transmitted to offspring.
2. Levy a birth tax on parents found to possess inferior genetic qualities likely to be transmitted to offspring.
3. Sterilize permanently at puberty all persons found to possess inferior genetic qualities likely to be transmitted to offspring.
4. Require genetic analysis tests as a basis for securing a marriage license. Where inferior genetic qualities are detected, no license will be issued until such time that both parties provide documented evidence that they have been sterilized.
5. Automatically abort all pregnancies conceived out of wedlock, with fines or imprisonment as penalties for the parents.
6. Require genetic analysis as a condition for granting passports for tourists wishing to travel to Mirania or for immigrants wanting to migrate to Mirania. Those found to possess inferior genetic qualities will not be permitted to enter the country.
7. Require all females who reach the age of thirty-five to be sterilized or to automatically terminate all pregnancies conceived after this age, since genetic defects are more likely to occur in offspring conceived by females who have reached this age.
8. Abort all fetuses found to possess transmittable genetic defects, or destroy at birth all babies found to possess physical defects or mental abnormalities due to genetic or environmental causes.
9. Deport or confine all individuals capable of transmitting inferior genetic qualities to an offspring.
10. Issue pregnancy permits allowing three children to those parents likely to transmit superior genetic qualities to offspring and allowing only one child to those unlikely to transmit superior genetic qualities.
11. Drop all government assistance to institutions and organizations that seek to maintain the life of individuals possessing mental or physical defects due to genetic causes.
12. Enable parents, relatives, or doctors to secure euthanasia permits to relieve the personal and social consequences of keeping alive the genetically inferior or mentally or physically defective.
13. Provide annual tax incentives for parents who possess inferior genetic qualities likely to be transmitted to offspring and who avoid conceiving children.

POPULATION CONTROL SUBCOMMITTEE REPORT FORM

Based upon genetic knowledge, the three policies that should become law are:

1. ______________________________

____

2. ______________________________

____

3. ______________________________

____

Based upon genetic knowledge, the three policies that should not be considered further are:

1. ______________________________

____

2. ______________________________

____

3. ______________________________

____

The grounds for selecting the first group of three as desirable policies are:

____

____

____

____

____

The grounds for selecting the last group of three as undesirable policies are:

____

____

____

____

____

In Pursuit of the General Welfare

Three other policies that should be given serious consideration at a later date are:

1. ______________________________

____

2. ______________________________

____

3. ______________________________

____

Signed: ____________________

____

____

____

____

CONSEQUENTIAL ANALYSIS GUIDE FOR RECOMMENDED POLICIES

Policy	Important Social Benefits of the Policy	Important Negative Consequences of the Policy
1. ______	1. ______	1. ______
	2. ______	2. ______
2. ______	1. ______	1. ______
	2. ______	2. ______
3. ______	1. ______	1. ______
	2. ______	2. ______

CONSEQUENTIAL ANALYSIS GUIDE FOR REJECTED POLICIES

Policy	Important Social Benefits of Rejecting This Policy	Important Social Costs of Rejecting This Policy
1. __________	1. __________	1. __________
	2. __________	2. __________
2. __________	1. __________	1. __________
	2. __________	2. __________
3. __________	1. __________	1. __________
	2. __________	2. __________

34. A Matter of Conception

TEACHER PREPARATION

1. Select five students to act as members of a decision-making panel.
2. Arrange seating so that the five members of the panel can be easily viewed by other members of the group as they seek consensus.
3. Secure sufficient copies of the situation for each member of the five-man decision-making panel. (You may wish to have enough copies to provide all class members with one.)
4. Send the five members of the panel into the hallway to rank order the alternatives from among which they are to make a decision.
5. While the panel members are in the hallway, instruct other members of the class that, as a result of listening and watching the decision-making group, they are to be prepared to answer such questions as:
   a. What decision was the group making? Under what conditions?
   b. To what degree and in what manner does this situation suggest that new scientific knowledge and shifting cultural values make once easy decisions difficult?
   c. What behaviors are vital to the successful operation of a decision-making group? (These are to be stated generally–abstractly–and not as a criticism of individual members of the panel.)
6. Decide whether you want to divide the entire class into small groups of four to six students. After having each student rank order his choices individually, have each group attempt to reach a consensus.

Social and Scientific Context

The local hospital in your community has been flooded with a number of requests for abortions. According to the law, members of the medical staff of the hospital can recommend cases for the consideration of a lay board of citizens; however, the final decision in each instance is to be determined by the lay board. How the lay board arrives at its decision is a matter that it can determine for itself. There is one rule: The panel must conduct its business in the open, where interested citizens can observe but cannot participate.

You have agreed to serve as a member of an abortion board. You and your colleagues have to determine, from among nine requests for an abortion, those that are deserving. Your panel has already met once in open hearing and agreed that you will arrive at your decision in three steps:

First, each member will individually rank order the requests from those that are most deserving to those that are least deserving. The best reason for an abortion is to be marked with a "1," the next best reason with a "2," and so on until the worst reason is marked with a "9." You are to rank order your list without consulting other members of the panel; to violate this rule would be to violate the sunshine rule, under which you are required to operate by law.

Second, you have agreed that the full panel will then seek consensus about granting three requests for abortion and denying three others. Three of the pregnant females involved will be allowed an immediate operation; three others will have their request denied until further justification or more evidence is available.

Third, you will deal with the three remaining applications in another meeting.

A Matter of Conception

At this stage, then, you are a member of a panel, meeting in an open session, with interested citizens observing how you make your decisions about the following applications:

1. The pregnant female possesses a blood disorder. This disorder, called embolism, takes the form of blood clotting. Her physician estimates that should she bear the child her chances of survival are 50-50.
2. The pregnant female, it is suspected, has been impregnated by an older brother. This relationship is called incest. Inasmuch as the mother's family and neighbors are members of a fundamentalist Protestant sect, the child, if born, will be perceived as a symbol of sin and evil.
3. The pregnant female is married to an unemployed laborer. She has difficulty feeding, clothing, and providing for the three children to whom she has already given birth. In addition, she and her husband subscribe to the work ethic and view the need to accept charity as evidence of their worthlessness.
4. The pregnant female and her husband possess a chromosomal abnormality. Using their genetic histories, her physician estimates that the odds are 60-40 that a full-term pregnancy and birth will eventuate in a mongoloid child.
5. The pregnant female, the mother of two children, is a social leader in the community. She is an active member, serving either as an officer or on the board of directors of such organizations as Community Chest, the League of Women Voters, Zero Population Growth, Central High School Band Boosters Club, and a women's liberation group called NOW. She argues that she has the personal right to use her body as she sees fit in order to continue to pursue social purposes beneficial to the community.
6. The pregnant female is married to a prominent local attorney who does not want another child. The pregnant female is already the mother of two adolescents—one a junior in high school and the other a freshmen in college. The parents seek an abortion claiming that another child will make it impossible for them to provide the two adolescents the education they have already planned.
7. The pregnant female has been found guilty of manslaughter in the death of a former child. She has refused to consider giving birth to the child and allowing it to be adopted.
8. The pregnant female, sixteen years old, was engaged in petting with her boyfriend. They went further than they had intended and pregnancy resulted. The parents of the couple have refused to give their consent for marriage, and they have filed a joint request for an abortion in the interest of their children.
9. The pregnant female, a nineteen-year-old college student, was picked up and raped by three boys while hitchhiking to class.

DECISION SHEET A

The three applications that should be approved are:

1.

2.

3.

Comments:

The results that I would hope for in allowing these abortions are (try to list three results for each application allowed):

DECISION SHEET B

The three applications that should be rejected are:

1. ______

2. ______

3. ______

Comments: ______

The harmful consequences of rejecting these applications are (try to list three consequences for each application rejected): ______

A Matter of Conception

Discussion Starters

1. What reasons for abortion did the panel consider?
2. How did the panel work? Under what conditions?
3. How should decisions of this sort be made?
4. Which females should have been allowed an abortion? Denied it?
5. Suppose you had approved an abortion and were asked to witness the operation. Would you accept the invitation? How would you feel as you watched?

35. Mirror, Mirror, on the Wall

TEACHER PREPARATION

1. **Secure sufficient copies of the value sheet for each student who will participate in the value clarification activity.**
2. **Decide whether you wish to place students in small groups and require consensus or to ask each student to respond individually.**
3. **Adjust the discussion starters to the content that you are teaching.**
4. **Determine whether or not you need to provide further information with regard to how individuals use other persons in order to define themselves.**

Social and Scientific Context

Socrates taught that the essence of human wisdom is to know thyself. Talking with other persons whom one values is one of the primary means that a person has for discovering who he is. When one is interacting with persons whose opinions and good regard he values, he uses the reactions of these persons as a mirror. By reacting to him, these persons provide him with feedback about the consequences of his opinions and values and help him to decide who he is as a person.

Different persons choose different people to serve as their mirrors. This choice, in turn, influences how they define themselves and who they become. Here are ten different persons with whom you might interact in order to define yourself as a person. Rank order these persons from the one you would most prefer to help you become the person you want to be, to the one you would least prefer to help you. To rank order these items, place a "1" beside the person whose influence you would most prefer, a "2" beside the person whose influence you would next prefer, and so on until you have placed a "10" beside the person whose influence you would least prefer.

_____ It is best to know thyself by talking to a person of your own age who is not necessarily your closest friend.

_____ It is best to know thyself by talking to your personal doctor.

_____ It is best to know thyself by seeking out and talking with a person from a different culture.

_____ It is best to know thyself by talking with your minister, rabbi, priest, or other religious leader.

_____ It is best to know thyself by seeking to talk with a person you have not met before.

_____ It is best to know thyself by talking with your brother or sister.

_____ It is best to know thyself by talking to your school guidance counselor.

_____ It is best to know thyself by talking with your father or mother.

_____ It is best to know thyself by talking with your closest friend.

_____ It is best to know thyself by talking with one of your teachers.

When you have rank ordered each item from "1" to "10," proceed to complete the decision sheets provided.

Mirror, Mirror, on the Wall

DECISION SHEET 1

The three persons with whom it is best to interact are:

1. ____________________

2. ____________________

3. ____________________

Good consequences likely to follow the selection of these three persons are:

1. ____________________

2. ____________________

3. ____________________

4. ____________________

Bad consequences likely to follow the selection of these three persons are:

1. ____________________

2. ____________________

3. ____________________

4. ____________________

DECISION SHEET 2

Of the persons listed, I am least likely influenced by the following:

1. ______________________________

2. ______________________________

3. ______________________________

The good consequences I might lose by failing to interact with these three persons are:

1. ______________________________

____

2. ______________________________

____

3. ______________________________

____

4. ______________________________

____

The advantages I gain by not interacting with these persons are:

1. ______________________________

____

2. ______________________________

____

3. ______________________________

____

4. ______________________________

____

Mirror, Mirror, on the Wall

Discussion Starters

1. What does the phrase "know thyself" mean?
2. How can a person learn who he is by going to school?
3. How can a person learn who he is by participating in social events?
4. Explain the statement, "School is concerned with *instruction.* The person is *educated* by his society and by his culture."
5. How might one use the ideas in this value sheet to justify the study of a foreign language? Of psychology?
6. Suppose you wished to argue for school integration and against school segregation. If you did, how could you organize the ideas in this value sheet to support such a position?
7. How should a person choose his acquaintances and friends?
8. When people with whom you are talking are critical of your ideas and opinions, what are your first feelings? What should you feel under these circumstances?
9. Should learning be an individual or a social matter? Explain.

36. The Governor Will Address the People

TEACHER PREPARATION

1. **Secure sufficient copies of the value sheet for each class member.**
2. **Help students to read and comprehend the situation before they begin independent work. At the end of the situation, the value sheet is marked by this direction: "Do not proceed past this point until instructed to do so." During this phase, students describe the situation in terms of its elements and relate these elements to the focus of study.**
3. **Decide (by group discussion if you wish) whether individual responses will later be shared with other members of the class. If they are to be shared, determine the form of the sharing experience. Be sure that students are informed about these matters before they commit themselves.**
4. **After students have comprehended the situation and have determined what they will do with the products of their individual effort, supply each with a "legislative adviser work sheet." (This is provided as part of the value sheet.)**

Social and Scientific Context

For this exercise in decision making, you are asked to assume that you are a close personal friend and political adviser to the governor of your state. This provides you with an opportunity to shape the policies and directions of social, economic, and political change in your state. The governor has just won re-election to office with more than 65 percent of the popular vote. A number of state legislators have gained office for the first time, riding the tide of popular approval for the governor. While these new legislative members feel obligated to the governor and expect him to recommend legislation consistent with his philosophy, more experienced legislators who would normally disagree with him are reluctant to risk confrontations with a governor who has received a popular mandate to continue his policies. This means, you assume, that quite often the governor will ask you to draft legislative proposals in the form of bills enabling legislators to transform his beliefs and commitments into law. Overly simplified: The governor will decide, you will write, and the legislature will "rubber stamp."

Subsequent to the governor's re-election, a major issue has stolen newspaper headlines, aroused various groups to take militant stands, and perplexed the governor. In order to assess the health needs and resources of the state, the governor appointed and secured legislative funding for a blue-ribbon committee to identify health-related problems and to recommend their resolution. This committee has submitted its final report and has released copies of its final conclusions to the news media. Among its recommendations to the governor, the committee has approved the concept of euthanasia (mercy killing) and has recommended that legislation be drafted and passed legalizing the practice.

Legislators, ministers, newspapers, television commentators, and even the governor's appointed cabinet have split and assumed highly polarized positions on this issue. A moderate is hard to find. Some hail the recommendation as a signpost of humanistic enlightenment and cultural progress; others are equally certain that the recommendation signifies human depravity and that its enactment will result in a cultural decline, a weakening of positive social values, and a threat to individual well-being. The governor, open to and swayed by both camps, cannot resolve his beliefs in his own mind. He complains to you that since this issue has been raised he can't put his head on straight in the morning and that he finds himself unable to deal with other pressing matters with the vigor and clarity of thought he believes necessary.

The issue refuses to die or abate. Emotions become, if anything, more heated. This emotional climate keeps constant pressure on the governor. Legislators ask him his position in private conferences. Ministers preach sermons demanding that he recommend approval; others preach equally well-written and delivered sermons demanding that he condemn this recommendation. Three ladies have started a statewide hike to dramatize the sancity of life; three men have started a statewide march of their own to dramatize support for the committee's recommendation that mercy killing be allowed. The state medical association is discomforted and reports publicly that the debate is weakening the trust necessary for a satisfactory doctor-patient relationship among the critically and terminally ill. Individual physicians and nurses recommend a firm stand, some supporting and some opposing mercy killings. Terminally ill patients send telegrams, some supportive of and some critical of euthanasia. Letters, telegrams, telephone messages, editorials, and advisers engulf the governor in a flood of arguments and counterarguments. His closest personal and political advisers insist that he must act; that the office cannot remain silent. The governor concurs with the need for action, but his beliefs and disbeliefs remain confused.

As a friend and legislative adviser, you have been privileged to participate in a number of meetings between the governor and parties vitally concerned about the issue. These meetings have involved medical experts, religious leaders, political cronies, and others from all areas of the state.

As a result of the pressures for action and of the information gained through conferences, you and the governor have summarized the substance of these discussions into nine specific statements relevant to the issue of "death with dignity." (This list is reprinted here and you will have an opportunity to read it after you and your classmates have discussed the situation itself.)

At this point the governor tells you that he has made a decision. He has already requested, and obtained, prime time to make a statewide television and radio address this evening in the interest of the public welfare. He wants to deliver a message that will cool emotions and make discussion of the issue more deliberate and more rational. His decision, then, is that consensus on this issue should be sought on calmly debated rational grounds rather than on the emotional statements that have led to shrill denunciations, causing those who subscribe to different positions to refuse to listen to one another. In line with these intentions, he hands you the list of arguments you and he have compiled and asks you to complete an assignment within the next hour.

He wants you to help him locate the three most important and the three least important statements about the issue. In his speech, he also wants to identify the *basis* (his criteria) for indicating that three arguments are *most* important and another three arguments are *least* important. Finally, he wants to establish that the grounds for assigning high priority to some arguments and questioning the significance of others are consistent with one another. You leave the governor's office with five jobs to complete in order to fulfill your assignment:

1. You are to list the three most cogent and powerful arguments relevant to the issue of euthanasia.

2. You are to identify criteria (reasons) one can use to argue the importance of these three arguments as a group.
3. You are to list the three least cogent and weakest arguments relevant to the issue of euthanasia.
4. You are to identify the criteria that can be used to establish the relative unimportance of these points of view.
5. You are to explain the degree to which the criteria identified in points 2 and 4 are consistent with one another.

Remember: The governor wants to change the nature of the debate; he wants people to stop debating euthanasia as a policy and instead to debate the norms by which government should make decisions influencing the personal and social welfare of citizens.

DO NOT READ FURTHER UNTIL INSTRUCTED BY YOUR TEACHER TO DO SO.

Nine Arguments

Prior to the governor's assignment, you and he had summarized nine arguments relevant to the issue of mercy killing:

1. The taking of a life, any life, is a direct violation of God's Commandment, "Thou Shalt Not Kill."
2. Persons who cannot become physically or mentally normal, who have no potential for living a normal life, should not be allowed to live, because they place a burden on the living.
3. The cost of medical care today is too prohibitive to allow the continuance of a person's life when either the survivors are driven deeper into debt or medical institutions become intolerable consumers of tax dollars.
4. The real murderers, in the event that a "death with dignity" bill is passed, will be those who sanction the practice and enrobe it with the dignity of law.
5. Mercy killings are likely to lead to legalized murder. It is not unlike the grotesque genocide practiced by Nazi Germany under Hitler's philosophy of social welfare. There is nothing to prevent our society, once Pandora's box has been opened, from using this precedent to frame legislation legalizing the elimination of other people whom society decides to label "undesirable."
6. Death with dignity is possible, but only when the actual act through which death is effected is performed by the patient himself. This cannot be accomplished by others carrying out the request of the dying person.
7. In a civilized society, the law must be humane—humane for the departing as well as for the surviving. Unless the act of freeing a person from a death of misery and suffering is performed with appropriate social ritual, death with dignity is impossible.
8. In terms of a number of vitally important research questions, those who are dying should be used, with their permission, to further man's knowledge of man; knowledge of either a social or scientific nature can be gained and can give a measure of meaning and purpose to the act of dying.
9. To accept this form of death offers each person an honorable way of ending his life. Its use in other cultures (suicide in Eastern faiths and sects) has allowed man to die with pride and without damage to other persons or to social institutions, and without cultural disorganization.

It is from these nine statements that you are to fulfill the governor's assignment within the hour.

The Governor Will Address the People

LEGISLATIVE ADVISER WORKSHEET

Before the hour is out you must complete this sheet and place it on the governor's desk. Make your statement concisely and as clearly as you can for the governor.

The three most relevant statements about the issue are:

1. ______________________________

____

2. ______________________________

____

3. ______________________________

The criteria on which these statements can be judged as most relevant are: ______________________________

____

____

The three least relevant statements with regard to the issue are:

1. ______________________________

____

2. ______________________________

____

3. ______________________________

____

The criteria on which these statements can be called least relevant are: ______________________________

____

____

How consistent are the criteria by which an argument is judged germane and important with those criteria by which an argument is ranked as being among the least important?

____

____

____

____

____

____

____

____

The Governor Will Address the People

Discussion Starters

1. What courses of action were open to the governor?
2. How should a governor respond to an issue and a situation such as the one described in this episode?
3. To what degree does the search for criteria for decision making (for norms of social, cultural, and personal judgment) tend to defuse an emotional issue?
4. Are there many circumstances under which you would support mercy killings? If so, can you identify your criteria?
5. In your opinion, is death a scientific, a medical, a social, a political, or a legal concept? Explain your response.

PROTOCOLS

The classification format of the value sheet may be thought of as containing at least five interrelated but distinguishable elements:

1. A situation relevant to the unit of instruction and from which one can abstract a list of choices.
2. A list of homogeneous alternatives, usually nine to fifteen in number.
3. A set of specific instructions to students enabling them to group their responses into three sets—the three best choices, the three worst choices, and the remaining choices.
4. A decision sheet on which students can write their choices for the three best and three worst rankings with provisions for identifying the basis for classifying these choices.
5. A set of questions or discussion starters.

While the teacher may view the classification format to be nearly identical to the rank-order format, the grouping of the top and bottom rankings into "classes of choices" increases the complexity of student responses.

To develop and use value clarification activities consistent with the classification format of the value sheet, the teacher should

1. Clearly state the topic, idea, or theme he is teaching and with which the value sheet is to be related.
2. Identify, locate, or contrive a situation relevant to the instructional unit that can provide a frame of reference for the classification task.
3. Identify the focus of the classification activity to be used in this particular episode (is it to focus on possible policies, consequences, case examples, or preferences?).
4. Develop a list of nine or more homogeneous options relevant to the situation, trying to assure that all the options are nearly equal in attractiveness or unattractiveness.
5. Consider whether students are to rank order the options before they group them into a set of best options and a set of worst options.
6. Develop a set of clear directions for his students, instructing them to rank order the choices from best to worst.
7. Develop a decision sheet on which his students can write the following: the three best choices as a group, the good consequences anticipated because of these options; the bad consequences anticipated because of these options; and the criterion used for classifying these three options as best.
8. Develop a decision sheet—similar to the one cited above—for the three worst choices.
9. Determine whether students are to share their responses in small groups. (If so, the teacher must determine the directions he will need to give to group members.)
10. Prepare a list of discussion starters consistent with the comprehension, relational, and valuation phases of value clarification.
11. Consider how he will make the transition from this activity in his instructional unit to the next activity he plans to use.

Teachers following these general procedures can develop value sheets in the classification format. Using the classification format, they can design and employ value clarification episodes that will enable students to generalize their value orientations within an ongoing instructional unit.

CHAPTER EIGHT

THE CRITERION FORMAT OF THE VALUE SHEET

The valuation phase of value clarification has been defined as that phase during which students express preferential, consequential, criterial, imperative, and emotive statements. Typically, the criterion format is designed to elicit and show interrelations among preferential, consequential, criterial, and imperative statements.

The criterion format contains a minimum of six elements. Of these, three have already been introduced. First, there is a social and scientific context establishing the conditions and the situation within which students are to work. Because of the complexity of the criterion format, this element contains a set of very specific directions as to how students are to respond to the value clarification episode. Second, there are decision sheets to guide students as they follow directions and respond to the value sheet. These are most helpful in assisting students to follow the directions incorporated as part of the social and scientific context. Third, there are follow-up questions consistent with the comprehension, relational, and valuation phases of value clarification. These three elements have been explained in conjunction with the other formats.

The criterion format contains three other elements. Each of these is to be thought of as a *universe*. That is to say, each element is complete—nothing of value or worth could be added to it. These three universes are a universe of policies, a universe of data, and a universe of criteria.

The *universe of policies* is a list of policies that can be used to resolve a problem situation provided by the social and scientific context. Students may be asked to select the best option, to rank order all options, or to classify options into classes of relative value. Students are confined to this list in order to stress that the options available to any decision-making group are always limited—sometimes by external restraints and sometimes by such internal constraints as limited knowledge or ideology.

The *universe of data* is a list of statements, all of which are to be presumed true for the time during which students are responding to a situation presented in the criterion format. This list may consist of empirical, interpretive, or consequential statements. Of these, the authors have found it most useful to use consequential statements. This list of statements is all the data with which the group can work. Once again, the intent is to underline that problem-solving groups operate under conditions of social and personal constraint. Not only is the range of policies limited, so is the range of data that a group can use.

The *universe of criteria* consists of a limited number of criterial statements, usually three to five. These statements are end values, such as survival, justice, freedom, equality, liberty, integrity, loyalty, law, and order. The three to five ideals are stated briefly; for example, "The best end that a person can seek is justice." However, these brief statements may be followed by an explanation of what the statement means. As was the case with the other two universes, the universe of criteria is complete. From this list students must select criteria on which to base their preferences or decisions.

The criterion format thus places students in a closed setting. Given a limited number of options, a limited amount of data, and a limited list of criteria, students must make decisions related to both the data and the criteria given. The effect is to obtain complex verbal responses associated with the valuation phase of value clarification.

SAMPLES

Value sheets written in the criterion format tend to be longer than value sheets written in other formats. For this reason, only three examples are presented in this section. These examples should provide you with an adequate opportunity to consider the six components of this format. An understanding of these components will anable you to comprehend and use the protocols that follow the three examples.

37. Company Man

TEACHER PREPARATION

1. **Study the value sheet until you are familiar with its components. A criterion value sheet contains a number of elements: a situation and set of directions; a list of alternative policies; a list of criteria from which a basis for deciding among policies is to be selected; a universe of data, often stated as known or anticipated consequences; and decision guides.**
2. **Decide whether you wish to have each student complete the value sheet or whether you wish to organize students into groups of four or five. (The latter works best.) If you opt to use small groups, ask each group to select one person to complete the decision sheets.**
3. **Make sure that students understand each element before asking that they complete the assignment.**
4. **Develop tentative questions you can use to help students relate their experience with this activity to the unit you are teaching.**
5. **Consider the possibility of asking students to analyze the consequences of each policy.**

Social and Scientific Context

The end of the progressive era witnessed some gains for the American labor movement, exemplified by such federal attempts to control monopoly as the Clayton Act of 1914, which declared that trade unions were not a conspiracy or a monopoly in restraint of trade.

By 1915, twenty-five states had passed laws limiting the working day, while thousands of workingmen had gained the eight-hour day through trade union action. By 1919, child labor laws, for which labor had agitated for nearly a century, had been passed by thirty-eight states. In that year, Massachusetts enacted the first minimum-wage law. The next year saw eight other states adopting laws concerning minimum-wage restrictions. By 1915, thirty-five states had passed laws providing for workmen's compensation after industrial accidents, another of the ancient demands of labor. In the same year, Congress passed the LaFollette Seamen's Act, an important step in removing seamen from a life of near serfdom. Until the law was passed, the ship's captain had absolute power over the seamen, and quitting a job during a voyage was a criminal offense. The Adamson Act of 1915 was passed after a strike threat by railroad workers. This act gave interstate railway employees the eight-hour day and time and a half for overtime work.

Yet, despite the wage and hour gains registered by American workers during these years, their real wages–the ability to buy back the goods and products they produced–were lower in 1914 than during the 1890s. This was true with respect to unionized as well as nonunionized wage earners. In effect, increased wages were not adequate to keep up with the cost of living.

Although the labor movement had shown significant gains by the end of the progressive era, the gains did not indicate the degree of conflict and personal trials and suffering of those workers who were on the front line of the struggle for reforms and improvement. The working conditions of the laborers were miserable and unrewarding. For this activity, you are a worker at the Acme Cloth and Shoe Company plant. The conditions under which you work include:

1. Job insecurity.
2. Poor sanitary conditions.
3. Low wages.
4. Growing impersonalization as factories grow larger.
5. No contracts.
6. Competition from cheap immigrant labor.
7. A twelve- to fourteen-hour working day.
8. Six- and sometimes seven-day work weeks.
9. No retirement plan.
10. Few child labor laws and none for children over ten.
11. Few safety regulations or precautions.
12. No bargaining power for workers.
13. Few breaks for relaxation, rest, recreation, and lunch.
14. The monotony of routine labor tasks.
15. No protection from business owner's decisions affecting one's pay, job, and so forth.

You head a family of four. You are making enough at your present salary to put a few cents in your savings account each month as well as to make it unnecessary for your wife and children to work. However, you find that the cost of living has gone up about $5.00 a month, causing you to begin taking money from your savings. As if this were not enough, you return to work one morning to discover that the owner has reduced everyone's salary by one dollar a month to cover the additional costs of raw materials and shipping. You and your co-workers decide that it is necessary to take some action.

You and a few of your co-workers are asked to explore what actions might be taken and to recommend what employees should do. The task of your committee is only to recommend; however, it is likely that your friends will follow the advice of the committee. Therefore, you and other members of the committee list alternatives, list harmful consequences that might as well be faced, and identify different arguments that could be used to justify your actions.

Of the alternatives available, your committee had decided that one of the following policies is to be recommended:

Policy A — Workers can engage in *boycotting* practices. This means that you, your family, and your friends will not buy the products made by the company until your demands for higher wages have been met. You may even try to convince others to do likewise.

Policy B — Workers can go on *strike*. This means that you will not only stop your work, but you will actively attempt to persuade others to do so. If necessary, you will compel others to stop working for the company.

Policy C — Workers can *resign*. This means that you will no longer report to work. It means that you have decided that you will refuse to work and will seek employment elsewhere. This is an individual rather than a group demonstration of protest or discontent.

Policy D — Workers can commit acts of *violence* and *sabotage* against the company. These activities are deliberate efforts to damage and destroy the owner's property. It is a massive attempt to cause the destruction of the company.

Policy E — Workers can engage in a work *slowdown*. This means that you will stay on the job but will reduce the amount of work you do so the production levels are

Company Man

lower. This is not a work stoppage, but a deliberate move to slow down production. This would, in effect, reduce the quantity of production without risking one's job, as a strike might tend to do.

The following consequences can reasonably be feared if the policies listed are adopted. Each policy that your committee might recommend will probably result in some harmful effects to each worker. These effects must be justified by appeal to some basis in the criteria given, as well as by weighing these negative effects against the positive results of the policy your committee recommends. Likely negative results are:

1. You can be fired.
2. You may be arrested.
3. You may have to look for another job.
4. The owner may lock you out of the company plant.
5. Scabs may be hired to replace you.
6. Strikebreakers may be hired to beat you up.
7. You may be fined in the courts.
8. The owner may sell the plant.
9. Federal troops may be called in to force you to work.
10. You may find that no other jobs are available and become unemployed.
11. You may get hurt or killed during demonstrations and protest activities.
12. Your wife may have to go to work.
13. Your children may have to drop out of school and work full time.
14. Prices for cloth and shoes may go up.
15. You may have to use your small savings account.
16. You may have to kill someone or hurt them as part of your protest activities.
17. You may be sent to jail.
18. The company may go bankrupt.
19. You may be accused of committing acts of violence.
20. You may be accused of being a "hypocrite" for taking a position different from what you have publicly stated.
21. You may be forced to borrow money, despite high interest rates.
22. The owner may lower the quality of his products.
23. The owner may have to decrease your salary even more to pay the costs of protection for his plant and to cover the loss of income due to the loss of products to sell.
24. You may have to find another job to supplement your lowered income and risk being fired from both if you are caught.

The criteria appropriate to make the decision are limited to these four:

1. The greatest good is to be found in *unity*. You have always been inspired by the old adage, "United we stand, divided we fall." At this time you are committed to the belief that, as a united body of employees, you are stronger and more likely to have your demands met. Your firm belief that there is strength in numbers is consistent with your past behaviors in town activities and in the company. You have expounded that a union of co-workers is a "union bound with blood, sweat, and tears." You have little sympathy for those who "desert the cause" and who refuse to remain with the group.
2. The greatest good is to be found in *loyalty*. You have worked for the company for all your working life. You have never earned a dime from any other employer. You have always regarded the owner as a "father to his employees" and have praised his kindliness and generosity in church and civic activities. You have always been faithful to him and have gone through a number of previous "crises." You have weathered them all. You feel you have always been "treated right" by the owner. Your loyalty has often shown itself in the amount of bragging you do about the company's products.
3. The greatest good is to be found in *survival*. There is a point in time that a person really becomes concerned about where his next meal will come from and who will pay the rent. You believe that, while many things are frills and unnecessary, there are some basic essentials a man needs for himself and his family. A man should not wait until his last penny is spent before he admits he is hungry and goes looking for something to eat. There are only a few jobs available, and those who hold them, whatever the salary, will eventually survive. The natural laws of evolution in society support this claim. Those that are without jobs are without salaries. They will eventually die. That is as it should be since they have proved themselves unfit to survive. Those who stick to a job without trying to improve their income and life may be clinging to a sinking ship. The struggle for survival will be won by those few who have earned the right to survive.
4. The greatest good is to be found in *pride*. You have often told your children and your fellow employees that to take away a man's pride is to take away his life. You have always been extremely proud of your work, your family, and your personal integrity. You have constantly put in extra time and energy at the company to make sure you did your job right. You have bragged to the whole community about the fine family you have and about the hospitality of your home. You have always been proud of your reputation and work.

DECISION SHEET

The best policy is: ____________________

____

____

The basis for selecting this action is the criterion that says: ____________________

____

____

The good consequences hoped for are: ____________________

____

____

____

____

The five negative consequences that are to be feared are: ____________________

____

____

____

____

____

____

____

If asked to justify these risks, I would use the criterion that says: ____________________

____

____

Company Man

Discussion Starters

1. To what degree is the man in this story a "company" man? To what degree is he a family man? To what degree is he a capitalist? To what degree is he an individualist?
2. Assuming that this man does depict the American worker during the progressive era, why would it be difficult to organize unions? Why would it be difficult to develop a union loyalty?
3. Did you identify the same criterion to select a policy that you used to justify negative consequences? If not, explain your failure to be consistent.

38. Genetics: Godly or Satanic Pursuit?

TEACHER PREPARATION

1. Secure copies of the value sheet for each student. This value sheet has the following components: (a) a set of directions that should be presented on a separate sheet; (b) a group of possible public policies related to the use of genetic knowledge; (c) a long list of social consequences that might be anticipated as effects of genetic breakthroughs; (d) a set of criteria statements (grounds) on which policies are to be selected; and (e) a worksheet on which students are to record and save their work. Because students will need to manipulate these components as they complete this task, distribute the elements separately and explain what each contains before distributing the next piece. (Once students have become accustomed to using this format, this amount of deliberateness and teacher-imposed structure will become less necessary.)
2. Identify vocabulary words likely to cause difficulty for your students and develop a glossary (on ditto or on the board).
3. After all five pieces of the value sheet have been distributed, divide students into decision groups with a minimum of five participants in each. Encourage students to first read the entire value sheet, then to spend the remainder of the first instructional period sharing ideas and making sure that they understand their assignment.
4. For each group either appoint or ask members to choose:
   a. A chairman, whose responsibilities are to make certain that the group focuses on the directions and to make sure that the group fulfills its task.
   b. A recorder, whose primary responsibilities are to keep a record of how the group performs and to fill in his group's worksheet as their work progresses.
   c. A participant whose primary focus is on possible social consequences and what is meant by each in the list.
   d. A participant whose primary focus is on the list of policies from which the group is to choose those that they would support.
   e. A participant whose primary focus is on the list of alternative criteria from which the group is to identify a basis for each policy they choose.
5. Decide whether you want students to fulfill the entire assignment as provided or whether they should just select the best policy.
6. Expect to use one day helping a group new to this format to understand and comprehend the materials and their assignment. A second day will probably be required for students to work their way through the materials and to build their decision sheets. If you wish to allow groups to share ideas formally, at least a portion of a third day will be necessary.

Directions

1. Make sure that all members understand all directions and all elements of this learning task before you start working. Stay calm and work carefully through each step. By the time you finish one or two explaining activities, you will be much more comfortable with it and will be able to risk shortcuts without risking failure.
2. From the list provided, select the policy that you would most prefer to see the United States adopt with regard to the use of genetic knowledge. This is the policy that your group agrees on as most preferable.
3. Once you have identified the most preferable policy to your group, identify the good (positive) consequences that you would expect to follow from its adoption. Then identify the bad (negative results) your group is willing to accept if it adopts this policy. Help your recorder to record this work on your decision sheet.
4. Having explored the consequences of the policy you selected as most preferable, identify the one criterion statement that is the single best basis for your policy.
5. Before proceeding, examine, as a group, whether or not your criterion is consistent with your policy and with the consequences you identified.
6. Proceed to select the second most preferable policy. Identify its consequences, locate the best criterion on which you can ground your policy, and make sure, again, that the policy, the consequences you have identified, and the ground for making your decision are consistent with one another.
7. Select the third most preferable policy and proceed as you did in direction 6.
8. Select the worst of the seven possible policies, identify its consequences, and choose one criterion statement that will support your contention that it is the worst of the policies listed.
9. Help your recorder make certain that he has an accurate record of the decisions your group has made. If he has, each member should sign it to signify that he believes it to be an accurate account.
10. Discuss how you worked together as a group and how you might improve your performance the next time you are working with a similar task.

Policies

1. Citizens should insist that their legislators support the work of genetic scientists if and only if the work of these scientists is directed at the detection, correction, or destruction of defective genes. Once this knowledge is secured, citizens should insist that their legislators pass laws requiring that persons known or suspected to have defective genes submit themselves to genetic surgery or to other recommended procedures likely to protect society from persons possessing defective genes.
2. Citizens should encourage their legislators to support scientists committed to the study of cloning. These scientists should be encouraged to duplicate creative artists, scientists, thinkers, and leaders. They should also have adequate support to observe and study their creations to determine whether reproduction by cloning also maintains and conserves the creativity of the persons "copied" by cloning.
3. Scientists should create unique humanoid creatures capable of living and studying in environments hostile to mankind. Such creatures could explore the sea and deep space more effectively than man. Since space and the ocean are man's last frontiers, they must be opened up for exploration, for exploitation, and possibly for settlement.
4. Citizens should create a lobby to support legislation designed to screen out and prevent genetically defective adults from participating in the conception of children. The legislation should require all persons applying for a marriage license to

present proof of genetic analysis as well as of a blood test. Where the male is found to have genetic defects, he should be required to submit to permanent sterilization—any children conceived in his marriage should be the product of artificial insemination. The female, if she has no genetic defects, should be required to sign two affidavits. In the first, she would commit herself to accept artificial insemination at a publicly controlled center, using sperm with the characteristics of the donor carefully detailed. In the second, she would formally sign an agreement to the effect that children so conceived would be made available to scientists for testing and study in order to advance genetic knowledge. Where both parties are defective, marriage licenses should be denied unless both parties present proof of sterilization.

5. Citizens should push scientists to take immediate steps to correct the problem of genetic loading. Since medical advances have maintained the life of individuals who would have died in the past and have thereby contributed to the polluting of the human genetic pool, the new frontier of genetic science should stress the discovery and use of means for removing undesirable traits from the genetic pool.
6. Citizens should immediately support legislation by which criminals serving life sentences for crimes of passion could volunteer as subjects for genetic experiments and genetically relevant research. After a number of such experiments and studies, graded according to risk, these individuals should be freed in return for their services to humanity. Prior to their release, these individuals would need psychiatric clearance insuring that they do not constitute a risk to society.
7. Citizens should support studies, institutes, and clinics in order to encourage the development of machines capable of duplicating the womb environment of the female. Parallel with these efforts, scientists should continue to seek synthetic substances to replace the human cell as a means for reproducing life. This will enable man to reproduce his species without risking defects attributable to such factors as genetic loading and radiation. It will also free women from their role as childbearer and homemaker and make them more equal.

Possible Consequences of Genetic Knowledge That Can Be Anticipated

1. Elimination of all hereditary disease and deformities from the human race.
2. Creation of a "super race" possessing those characteristics deemed most essential for human beings to possess.
3. Development of an elite class of superior individuals, especially bred to fulfill vital leadership roles in society.
4. Creation of specialized classes of individuals bred for such specific social functions as research, recreation, service industries, accounting, and so forth so that all workers engage in jobs for which they are fitted.
5. Duplication of individuals dangerous to mankind—Hitler, Stalin, and so forth.
6. Duplication of individuals helpful to mankind—Salk, King, Pericles, and so forth.
7. Duplication of superstars who would dominate different sports and be bred especially for basketball, football, wrestling, archery, bowling, tennis, and baseball.
8. Preservation of the life, thought, and moral influence of individuals victimized by untimely accidents and assassinations—for example, the Kennedy brothers or the Gracchi.
9. Population control and zero growth.
10. Elimination of male and female sexual stereotypes.
11. Preservation of reproductive cells (sperm) for eventual emergency use.
12. Alteration in the meaning of such words as "born," "life," "death," "human," "father," and "mother."
13. Modification of religious faiths and conceptions about God.
14. Introduction of the concept of property rights as a sexual question.
15. Alteration of contemporary laws relating to individual rights to life, due process, privacy, equal protection, and so forth.
16. Preservation of human life for two, three, or more centuries.
17. Replacement of money bankers by genetic bankers in prestigious positions (such as on school boards).
18. Elimination of individuals currently draining resources of the state.
19. Appearance of a class society made up of two castes: humans, born of human parents, and humanoids, produced in the laboratory.
20. Production increases in agricultural products through cloning.
21. Organization of alternative schools to socialize and educate different kinds and types of human beings.
22. Creation of a climate in which atomic warfare (now unthinkable according to some because of the effects of radiation on genes) would be quite acceptable, since man's genetic ability to reproduce would be possible regardless of radiation level.
23. Creation of a meritocracy.
24. Rejection of science by society.
25. Increased efforts by science to control the human mind as effectively as it can now control the human body.
26. Creation of a more humane, ethical, and moral society.
27. Emergence of a totally planned society.
28. A revolution in veterinary medicine.
29. Revision of the Hippocratic oath as a code of ethics for doctors and nurses.
30. Replacement of contemporary man with "future man."
31. Elimination of pain and suffering due to diseases now common to the human race.
32. Reduction in the risk of birth defects for children born of men and women in high-risk professions, such as radiologists, astronauts, and x-ray technicians.
33. Disappearance of human freedom as we now know it.
34. Incorporation of genetic counseling into sex education classes.
35. Elimination of all value we place on human life.
36. Alteration of intelligence scores for the human species.
37. Creation of class warfare between "human-humans" and "created-humans."
38. Creation of greater need for genetic counselors.
39. Transformation in the major role of hospitals and medical centers.
40. Creation of a humanoid "slave class" to do the difficult and dirty jobs now being done by human beings.

Genetics: Godly or Satanic Pursuit?

Criterial Statements

1. Man is a gregarious and social animal who lives and survives in groups. The individual must submit to rules, regulations, and procedures that serve the interests of his total society. To do less is to be selfish, antisocial, and antiman.
2. Science cannot and should not concern itself with the religious beliefs and conventional faiths of a particular time and place. The purpose of science is to discover new knowledge and to predict the future.
3. As far as we know, man is the only creature in the universe who is aware of himself as having once "not been" and of facing a time when he will "no longer be." His highest ethic must be to preserve and protect himself as a species. His highest moral responsibility is to protect those who will follow him–his posterity.
4. The pursuit of scientific knowledge cannot be restricted. Without the continued freedom to search where they will and to perform necessary experiments, scientists will be unable to function and science will die. With the death of the spirit of scientific inquiry, we will rapidly lose our individual freedoms, our sense of personal dignity and worth, and our ability to progress. Society as we know it will wither and decay.

Genetics: Godly or Satanic Pursuit?

DECISION SHEET 1

(Note to recorder: Please attempt to express ideas in the words used by members of your group. Do *not* copy the statements of policy, of consequences, or of criteria.)

The most preferable policy is: ______

______

______

______

______

If challenged to justify this policy and to provide a reason for accepting its negative consequences, the best criterion statement is: ______

______

______

______

______

Anticipated positive consequences of this policy (benefits for man as a species) are: ______

______

______

______

______

Anticipated negative consequences of this policy are: ______

______

______

______

______

DECISION SHEET 2 (optional)

The second most preferable policy is: ______________________________

If challenged to support this policy and to provide a reason for accepting its negative consequences, the best criterion statement is: ______________________________

Anticipated positive consequences of this policy (benefits for man as a species) are: ______________________________

Anticipated negative consequences of this policy are: ______________________________

DECISION SHEET 3 (optional)

The third most preferable policy is: ____________________

If challenged to justify this policy and to provide a reason for accepting its negative consequences, the best criterion statement is: ____________________

Anticipated positive consequences of this policy (benefits for man as a species) are: ____________________

Anticipated negative consequences of this policy are: ____________________

Genetics: Godly or Satanic Pursuit?

Discussion Starters

1. To what degree is the science of genetics likely to influence contemporary American society? Future American society?
2. To what degree is the nature of Western society (especially in America) likely to influence the development of the science of genetics?
3. Will the scientist who is associated with genetics come to be perceived as a godly figure? Explain your response.
4. If it is acceptable or "good" that scientists can alter heredity, are there any areas of human existence that should be off-limits to the scientist?
5. Might society be considered "good" if it prevented the scientist from experimenting in the area of genetics?
6. To what degree does man need to be aware of his ancestors in making decisions affecting the human beings of the future? Should this awareness limit his efforts to affect his descendents through applying genetic knowledge?

All together now...
DIXIE!

39. The Tardy Bell

TEACHER PREPARATION

1. **Organize students in small groups of four to five participants.**
2. **Distribute a copy of the value sheet to each student who is participating in the value clarification activity.**
3. **Help students to familiarize themselves with each of the following elements: (a) a set of directions; (b) a set of eight policies; (c) a universe of descriptive data; (d) a set of three value norms; and (e) a set of decision sheets on which students are to keep a record of their work.**
4. **Encourage students to closely follow the directions provided.**
5. **Determine how you will assist students to relate this exercise to the unit in which you decide to assign it.**

Social and Scientific Context

Several years ago the staff and student body of Rebel Rock High School were integrated pursuant to federal court orders. Initially, integration worked smoothly. Although blacks tended to associate with blacks and whites tended to associate with whites, little friction or tension was observable in the situation. However, for the last two years Rebel Rock High School has been the scene of an annual interracial disturbance. In addition, the frequency of confrontations between blacks and whites has risen dramatically. Over the years a number of policy changes that might ease tensions and help students and teachers work together cooperatively have been suggested to a biracial committee whose functions it has been to make integration work. Faced with a rising tide of violence that threatens the total instructional situation, the biracial committee is forced to consider acting on policies it has previously ignored. The biracial committee has appointed a subcommittee to consider each policy recommendation and to report back to the full committee. For purposes of this activity, you are to consider yourself a member of this subcommittee.

The subcommittee is to consider eight policies that have been recommended to the total biracial committee. Your subcommittee is to recommend or reject each of the eight policies. The steps you are to follow in undertaking this task are:

1. Make sure each member of your subcommittee understands what is meant by each of the eight policies given.
2. Make sure that each member of your subcommittee understands each item of information given in the descriptive data.
3. Make sure that each member of your subcommittee understands each of the three value norms on the basis of which policies are to be recommended for adoption or rejection.
4. Use the understandings developed with regard to the eight policies, the universe of descriptive data, and the value norms in order to complete the decision sheets provided.

Policies Being Acted on by the Biracial Advisory Committee of Rebel Rock High School

1. The school will not change its name; however, all symbolism associated with its name and with the traditions of the Confederacy, upon which the symbolism is based—school colors, band uniforms, school flag, the "rebel yell," the playing of "Dixie," and portraits of Confederate leaders and generals such as Lee, Stuart, Davis, and Longstreet—will be replaced by new symbols and traditions that will not offend blacks.
2. The school's symbols and traditions are so much a part of the history and spirit of the school that they will be maintained regardless of opposition to the contrary.
3. The school's administration, faculty, and student body will organize and sponsor a social group called the Black Student Union (BSU) and will restrict its membership to black students.
4. Any student who whistles or sings "Dixie," wears or carries any ensignia associated with the Confederacy, or waves or possesses a Confederate flag or fascimile on the campus or on the adjacent property will be expelled from the school for an indefinite period.
5. Teachers of American history will develop and teach units stressing the role of blacks in American history, and these units must emphasize the contributions and the benefits to America of the blacks. In addition, elective courses in black history, black culture, and black literature will be planned and offered as credit courses beginning next semester.
6. Any black student using symbolic gestures associated with "black power" or "antiwhitism" will be expelled immediately from the school for an indefinite period.
7. Instructional units that cover such areas as race relations, history, sociology, civics and government, and problems of democracy will treat black and white relations objectively; however, students will be encouraged to explore the consequences of situations being studied in terms of the social and personal implications they have on Americans, black and white.
8. Any administrator or teacher found giving rewards or privileges to students or depriving or punishing students because of their color, attitudes, or race-related behavior shall be suspended immediately.

Universe of Descriptive Data Relevant to the Rebel Rock Situation

1. Historically, American blacks have been deprived of social equality, civil rights, and equal opportunities.
2. During the first half of the twentieth century, whites have not respected the civil rights of blacks, and blacks have seldom exercised their rights.
3. American blacks have been forced to attend inadequately equipped schools staffed with teachers less skilled than those who teach whites.
4. The white American school has been a different and better social institution in which to obtain an education.
5. American blacks, aware that they have been victimized by an irrational prejudice, are often understandably enraged when whites appear to practice the same behaviors that were once closely associated with racism.
6. Psychologically, blacks of the past have internalized social prejudices at the expense of their pride and self-esteem.
7. The role of blacks in American history and culture remains an area of relative ignorance in the American mind.
8. In order to foster group pride, blacks have developed slogans and symbols in order to institutionalize and ritualize behavioral patterns associated with pride in oneself and in one's race and its cultural and historical heritage.
9. In America, it remains true that blacks are more likely to be unemployed, more likely to occupy fewer influential positions, and more likely to lose their jobs.

10. By law, blacks and whites must attend the same public school, attend common classes, and participate equally in cocurricular and extracurricular activities.
11. Blacks have become activists, seeking to create circumstances and procedures that will enable them to participate in the definition and pursuit of "the good life," formerly open only to whites.
12. Blacks seek their goals by varied strategies. Persuasion, nonviolent protests, violent protests, legislation, court orders, cultural renewal through black pride activities, and radical separatism are some of the options available to, and used by, adolescent and adult blacks.
13. White students at Rebel Rock High view integration apprehensively. They have never associated with blacks, and they fear the unknown. Most have subscribed to stereotypes.
14. Black students look forward with some apprehension to attending a white school. They fear whites, but they fear loosing their pride even more.

The Value Norms: The Criteria for Decision Making Available to the Committee

1. Integration of all Americans into one community is good; any drift or movement toward segregation is bad.
2. Desegregation, by which facilities and funds previously restricted to whites are available to all Americans, is good; however, efforts to achieve an integrated school community in which race is irrelevant is wrong.
3. Neither desegregation nor integration is desirable; separatism is best, but, because of certain ill-advised court decisions, it must be fostered within the desegregated school.

DECISION SHEET A

Should Policy 1 be adopted? _____ Yes _____ No

The data most relevant to your decision to adopt or to reject this policy are: ______________________

The best criterion on which your committee can base its decision with regard to this policy states: ______________________

DECISION SHEET B

Should Policy 2 be adopted? _____ Yes _____ No

The data most relevant to your decision to adopt or to reject this policy are: ______

The best criterion on which your committee can base its decision with regard to this policy states: ______

DECISION SHEET C

Should Policy 3 be adopted? _____ Yes _____ No

The data most relevant to your decision to adopt or to reject this policy are: ______________________________

The best criterion on which your committee can base its decision with regard to this policy states: ______________________________

DECISION SHEET D

Should Policy 4 be adopted? _____ Yes _____ No

The data most relevant to your decision to adopt or to reject this policy are: ______________________________

____

____

____

____

____

____

____

____

The best criterion on which your committee can base its decision with regard to this policy states: ______________________________

____

____

____

____

____

____

____

____

DECISION SHEET E

Should Policy 5 be adopted? _____ Yes _____ No

The data most relevant to your decision to adopt or to reject this policy are: ______________________________

The best criterion on which your committee can base its decision with regard to this policy states: ______________________________

DECISION SHEET F

Should Policy 6 be adopted? _____ Yes _____ No

The data most relevant to your decision to adopt or to reject this policy are: ____________________

The best criterion on which your committee can base its decision with regard to this policy states: ____________________

DECISION SHEET G

Should Policy 7 be adopted? _____ Yes _____ No

The data most relevant to your decision to adopt or reject this policy are: ____________________

The best criterion on which your committee can base its decision with regard to this policy states: ____________________

DECISION SHEET H

Should Policy 8 be adopted? _____ Yes _____ No

The data most relevant to your decision to adopt or to reject this policy are: ______________________________

The best criterion on which your committee can base its decision with regard to this policy states: ______________________________

The Tardy Bell

Discussion Starters

1. What function was assigned to the biracial committee of Rebel Rock High School?
2. When did the biracial committee of Rebel Rock High School decide to take action?
3. Benjamin Franklin taught that "a stitch in time saves nine." How do you explain the fact that the committee was so late in acting?
4. To take steps that will halt riots and curtail interracial incicents will solve the problem that faces the committee. To go further and remove the causes of interracial incidents would be to resolve the issues leading to riots and incidents. Which goal would you expect the biracial committee to pursue, problem solving or issue resolution? Why? With what effect?
5. Given your experience with this value sheet, to what degree can one base a policy decision on the facts?
6. If one cannot base a decision on the facts, what happens to the facts when one makes a decision?
7. Would you prefer to perceive yourself as a person who solves problems or as a person who resolves issues? Explain.

PROTOCOLS

The criterion format of the value sheet contains six distinct elements:

1. A social and scientific context relevant to the unit of instruction and including directions for completing the assignment.
2. A universe of policies, usually five in number, from which one policy is to be chosen.
3. A universe of data, sometimes twenty to thirty in number, that provides a list of information or consequences relevant to the situation.
4. A universe of criteria, usually three to five in number, that serves as the source for a criterion upon which a decision can be made.
5. A decision sheet to guide students as they complete the decision-making task presented in the episode.
6. A set of questions or discussion starters.

The six components of the criterion format render it more complex than any of the formats previously presented. However, once the teacher becomes familiar with this format, the components become less difficult to develop and to include in instructional units.

In order to write value sheets in the criterion format, the teacher should use the following directions as rules:

1. Prepare and use activities by which students can develop a good background relevant to the situation that you plan to stress in the value sheet episode. The criterion format is more useful as a culminating activity and therefore should be utilized toward the end of an instructional sequence.
2. Locate, contrive, or describe the context and establish its relevance to the unit of study you are planning. This context should include specific and detailed directions.
3. Identify a list of effects (good and bad) likely to eventuate if the contrived or described situation is allowed to continue without human intervention. This list should contain a minimum of twelve consequences. It should contain, in random order, a number of consequences the teacher believes his students would consider bad and others he believes they would consider good.
4. Preface the universe of data with a statement to the effect that, for purposes of the exercise, these data or consequences are a full universe, the only effects or data relevant to the situation are listed, and these effects or data are all true.
5. Identify a minimum of three criteria on which students are either to choose the best policy or to rank order the policies given.
6. Preface the page that contains these criteria with a statement to the effect that, for this exercise, students are to behave as if only these criteria are pertinent to the decision that is to be made.
7. Create a list of at least five policies, the selection of which will probably lead to some good consequences and, at the same time, will involve the sacrifice of certain good effects that would eventuate from other policy options.
8. Preface the page that contains these policies with a statement to the effect that, for purposes of this exercise, students are to assume that these are the only possible policies.
9. Develop a decision sheet that will help the student to state his choice from among policies, to state the good effects likely to result from his choice, to state the bad effects his choice indicates he is willing to accept or risk, and to identify the grounds on which he would argue that the bad effects risked are justified.
10. Write an overview of the exercise that provides the student with information about the five elements in this format of the value sheet: (a) a situation, complete with directions for the responding student or group; (b) a universe of data; (c) a universe of criteria to be used as the grounds for making a decision; (d) a list of policies from among which a decision is to be made; and (e) a decision worksheet. (If the policies are to be rank ordered, directions should be altered and a number of decision sheets provided.)
11. Plan or write the kinds of empirical, relational, valuing, and feeling questions you will use to guide a follow-up discussion relevant to the unit of work for which you are planning the value sheet.
12. Determine whether you want students to work first in small groups or as individuals. (If in small groups, you may wish to plan on making individual members responsible for different elements as the group cooperatively completes the decision sheet.)

When a teacher has comprehended these rules, he can plan and write value sheets in the criterion format. This ability will enable the teacher to help students use complex patterns of language that can be associated with value clarification. The teacher will certainly be prepared to begin using value clarification activities in order to help students learn and refine such skills as empathizing, deciding, and assenting. This is the *beginning* that was established as the *end* goal of *Value Clarification in the Classroom: A Primer.*

APPENDIX A

CHECKLISTS FOR CONSTRUCTING DIFFERENT FORMATS OF THE VALUE SHEET

When teachers write their own value sheets, they can focus them more directly on units they plan and teach and they can deliberately stress aspects of their local community as well as more general aspects of the context that they believe are most worth learning and applying. The checklists in this appendix are designed to guide teachers as they create their own value sheets.

CHECKLIST FOR THE STANDARD FORMAT

_____ 1. Have I clearly stated the topic, idea, or theme of my unit of instruction?

_____ 2. Have I identified the appropriate spot in my instructional unit to assign and discuss this value sheet activity?

_____ 3. Have I selected a learning resource relevant to my instructional unit that will serve as the focus of inquiry and value clarification? (The resource may be a cartoon, a poem, a selection from a novel or essay, a magazine or newspaper article, a picture, a graph, a chart, a demonstration, or an experiment. It may also be an abstract of any of these.)

_____ 4. Have I prepared two or three questions designed to help students comprehend and understand the learning resource I have selected? (These questions are designed to elicit student statements consistent with the comprehension phase of value clarification. They are attached to the learning resource and should be available on a separate sheet of paper, on the chalkboard, or on overhead transparencies so the students can respond in writing before the discussion begins.)

_____ 5. Have I prepared two or three questions designed to enable students to relate the learning resource and its relevant information to the topic, idea, or theme they are studying? (These questions are designed to elicit student statements consistent with the relational phase of value clarification.)

_____ 6. Have I prepared one to three questions designed to assist students in examining and expressing their values and feelings relative to the learning resource, topic, idea, or theme they are studying or to their own personal response to the value sheet activity? (These questions are designed to elicit student statements consistent with the valuation phase of value clarification.)

_____ 7. Have I secured enough copies of the learning resource and the list of questions or otherwise made provision for each student to read, observe, or listen to them?

_____ 8. Have I considered and made provisions for the preparation my students will need in order to use this value clarification activity?

_____ 9. Have I considered how I will make the transition from this activity in my instructional unit to the next activity I plan to use?

CHECKLIST FOR THE FORCED-CHOICE FORMAT

_____ 1. Have I clearly stated the topic, idea, or theme of my unit of instruction?

_____ 2. Have I identified the appropriate spot in my instructional unit to assign and discuss this value sheet activity?

_____ 3. Have I located a resource that describes a situation or provides a contextual setting relevant to the unit of instruction? (The resource can be abstracted from a magazine or newspaper article, a novel, a short story, or a historical incident, or it may be a contrived situation.)

_____ 4. Have I adopted or modified the resource to meet the requirements of my teaching unit and the specific needs of my students?

_____ 5. Have I abstracted from the resource, or from the situation presented by the resource, three to five possible alternatives applicable to a decision-making situation?

_____ 6. Have I framed and listed the three to five alternative choices to fit the contextual setting of the resource being used?

_____ 7. Have I made the alternative choices homogeneous? (All the choices should be nearly equal in attractiveness or unattractiveness. They should also be similar in that all should be policies, consequences, ideals, or preferences.)

_____ 8. Have I included adequate instructions to assist students in completing the forced-choice task?

_____ 9. Have I developed a decision sheet on which my students can identify their choice and state the basis used for making their decision?

_____ 10. Have I developed and written follow-up questions as discussion starters that will help students share their understanding of the resource, the situation, the list of alternatives, and the choices they made in response to the forced-choice task?

_____ 11. Have I included questions designed to elicit student statements consistent with the comprehension, relational, and valuing phases of value clarification?

_____ 12. Have I considered whether students are to share their responses in small group discussions? If so, have I prepared instructions for their small group discussion?

_____ 13. Have I secured enough copies of this value sheet or made adequate provision for each student to read, study, and complete the activities in it?

_____ 14. Have I considered how I will make the transition from this activity in my instructional unit to the next activity I plan to use?

CHECKLIST FOR THE AFFIRMATIVE FORMAT

_____ 1. Have I clearly stated the topic, idea, or theme of my unit of instruction?

_____ 2. Have I identified the appropriate spot in my instructional unit to assign and discuss this value sheet activity?

_____ 3. Have I located a resource or identified a situation that provides a contextual setting relevant to the unit of instruction? (This situation and setting may be based upon an actual event, abstracted from a play or novel, or they may be contrived especially for this activity.)

_____ 4. Have I adapted or modified the resource or contextual situation to meet the requirements of my teaching unit and the specific needs of my students?

_____ 5. Have I written the situation in such a way that it adequately describes the context within which students are to make their decision?

_____ 6. Have I identified the focus of the decision-making situation contained in this value clarification activity? (The decision-making situation is relevant to the idea, topic, or theme of the instructional unit.)

_____ 7. Have I modified the context so that students are placed in a problematic situation with a limited number of options available to them? (Each of these options possesses both attractive and unattractive features. Each of the options is reasonable given the conditions and situation presented in the context.)

_____ 8. Have I specified whether students are to make their decision on the basis of the greatest good of several possibilities or the least bad of several bad options?

_____ 9. Have I checked to ensure that an adequate amount of background information is provided to establish a frame of reference within which the students can operate and consider their decision?

_____ 10. Have I ended the problematic situation with the student having to make a decision and with emphasis on the fact that he is to make the best possible decision?

_____ 11. Have I included adequate instructions to assist students in completing this value clarification activity? (These instructions can conclude by taking the form of an incomplete sentence such as, "Given the situation in which I find myself, the best decision I can make is . . .")

_____ 12. Have I provided adequate space and made provision for enough time for students to examine the situation, make their decision, and write out their responses? (Five to fifteen minutes is an average amount of time to complete this step of the value sheet.)

_____ 13. Have I considered developing a separate decision or response sheet to fit both the context of the problematic situation and the nature of the response asked for in the value sheet? (The context may necessitate a separate, distinct response sheet, such as a telegram, a letter, or a ballot, to emphasize to students the seriousness of their decision.)

_____ 14. Have I developed and written follow-up questions that will help students share their understanding of the situation–and of the options available at the time of the decision–and to examine their decision and its possible ramifications?

_____ 15. Have I included questions designed to elicit student statements consistent with the comprehension, relational, and valuation phases of value clarification?

_____ 16. Have I considered whether students are to share their responses in small group discussions? If so, have I prepared instructions for their small group discussion?

_____ 17. Have I secured enough copies of the value sheet for each student to read, study, and complete the activities included in this value clarification episode?

_____ 18. Have I considered and made provisions for the preparation my students will need in order to use this value clarification activity.

_____ 19. Have I considered how I will make the transition from this activity in my instructional unit to the next activity I plan to use?

CHECKLIST FOR THE RANK-ORDER FORMAT

_____ 1. Have I clearly stated the topic, idea, or theme of my unit of instruction?

_____ 2. Have I considered the appropriate spots in my instructional unit to assign and discuss this value sheet activity?

_____ 3. Have I selected a situation that can provide a contextual setting relevant to the unit of instruction? (This situation may be abstracted from a story or from a historical or recent incident, or it can be invented.)

_____ 4. Have I adapted or modified the contextual situation to meet the requirements of my teaching unit and the specific needs of my students?

_____ 5. Have I identified and developed the situation so that it provides a frame of reference for the rank-order task? (The situation should be rewritten or modified to stress the context within which students are to perform the rank-order task.)

_____ 6. Have I identified the focus of the rank-order task to be used in this value clarification activity? (The task should focus on either consequences, policies, ideals, preferences, or interpretations.)

_____ 7. Have I developed a list of five to twelve homogeneous options for the rank-order task? (All the options should be nearly equal in attractiveness or unattractiveness. They should also be similar in that they should all be possible consequences, policies, ideals, preferences, or interpretations.)

_____ 8. Have I checked to see if the rank-order options and task are reasonable, given the conditions and situation presented in the context?

_____ 9. Have I checked to make sure the items to be rank ordered are properly introduced within the context of the value clarification situation?

_____ 10. Have I included a clear and specific set of instructions to assist students in the completion of the rank-order task? (The instructions should be similar to the following: "Mark the choice you like best with a '1,' your second choice with a '2,' your third choice with a '3,' and so forth until you have ranked all items.")

_____ 11. Have I left a space prior to each option of the rank-order task for students to indicate its rank as they assign value to it? (If necessary, assign numbers to avoid confusion during discussion.)

_____ 12. Have I determined whether a separate decision sheet is to be developed and included as part of this value clarification activity?

_____ 13. Have I developed and written follow-up questions (discussion starters) that will help students share their understandings of the situation and of the list of rank-order options?

_____ 14. Have I included questions designed to elicit student statements consistent with the comprehension, relational, and valuation phases of value clarification?

_____ 15. Have I considered whether students are to share their responses or to reach a consensus in small groups? If so, have I determined the directions I will need to provide group members?

_____ 16. Have I secured enough copies of this value sheet or made adequate provision for each student to read, study, and complete the activities included in it?

_____ 17. Have I considered and made provisions for the preparation my students will need in order to use this value clarification activity?

_____ 18. Have I considered how I will make the transition from this activity in my instructional unit to the next activity I plan to use?

CHECKLIST FOR THE CLASSIFICATION FORMAT

_____ 1. Have I clearly stated the topic, idea, or theme of my unit of instruction?

_____ 2. Have I identified the appropriate spot in my instructional unit to assign and discuss this value sheet activity?

_____ 3. Have I selected a situation that can provide a contextual setting relevant to the unit of instruction? (This situation may be abstracted from a novel or short story, a historical or fictional incident, or current news, or it can be invented.)

_____ 4. Have I adapted or modified the contextual situation to meet the requirements of my teaching unit and the specific needs of my students?

_____ 5. Have I identified and developed the situation so that it provides a frame of reference for the valuing task? (The situation should be rewritten or modified to stress the context within which students are to engage in the classification task.)

_____ 6. Have I identified the focus of the classification task to be performed during this value clarification activity? (The task should focus on either consequences, policies, ideals, preferences, or interpretations.)

_____ 7. Have I developed a list of nine or more homogeneous options for the classification task? (All the options should be similar in that they should all be possible policies, preferences, or consequences.)

_____ 8. Have I checked to see if the options are reasonable, given the conditions and situation presented in the context?

_____ 9. Have I checked to make sure the items to be classified are properly introduced within the context of the value clarification situation?

_____ 10. Have I included a clear and specific set of instructions to assist students in the completion of the grouping assignment?

_____ 11. Have I developed a separate decision sheet on which students can record their decisions and analyze their responses with regard to likely effects?

_____ 12. Have I determined whether it is best for students to complete the decision sheet individually or as members of small groups? If so, have I prepared instructions for their small group discussion?

_____ 13. Have I developed and written follow-up questions (discussion starters) that will assist students in sharing their understandings of the context and in examining their decisions, preferences, and feelings?

_____ 14. Have I included questions designed to elicit student statements consistent with the comprehension, relational, and valuation phases of value clarification?

_____ 15. Have I secured enough copies of the value sheet and its decision sheet(s) for each student to read, study, and complete the components included in this value clarification activity?

_____ 16. Have I considered and made provisions for the preparation my students will need in order to use this value clarification activity?

_____ 17. Have I considered how I will make the transition from this activity in my instructional unit to the next activity I plan to use?

CHECKLIST FOR THE CRITERION FORMAT

_____ 1. Have I clearly stated the topic, idea, or theme of my unit of instruction?

_____ 2. Have I identified the appropriate spot in my instructional unit to assign and discuss this value sheet activity?

_____ 3. Have I prepared and used activities in my instructional unit by which students have developed an adequate background of knowledge relevant to the situation stressed in this value sheet episode?

_____ 4. Have I selected a situation that can provide a contextual setting relevant to the unit of instruction? (This situation may be abstracted from a story or a historical account, or it can be invented.)

_____ 5. Have I adapted or modified the contextual situation to meet the requirements of my teaching unit and the specific needs of my students?

_____ 6. Have I identified and developed the situation so that it provides a frame of reference for the criterion task?

_____ 7. Have I determined whether the "universe of data" is to include possible consequences, factual information, or interpretations?

_____ 8. Have I identified and developed a list of alternatives relevant to my universe of data that fits the contrived or described situation found in the value clarification episode? (The list should contain homogeneous options in random order. All options should be either consequences, pieces of factual data, or interpretations.)

_____ 9. Have I identified and stated a minimum of three criteria to serve as the basis upon which students are to either choose the best policy or to rank order the policies given? (This set serves as the "universe of criteria.")

_____ 10. Have I identified and stated at least five policies each of which, if selected, will probably lead to some good consequences? (This set serves as the "universe of policies.")

_____ 11. Have I prefaced each universe of statements with a statement to the effect that, for purposes of this activity, this list is a full and true universe? (Only information relevant to the situation should be in-included, and the information should be true.)

_____ 12. Have I checked to see if the items in each of the sets are homogeneous?

_____ 13. Have I checked to make sure the separate sets of universes are properly introduced within the context of the value clarification situation? (The exercise should contain an overview that provides the student with information about five specific elements in this format: a situation complete with directions for the responding group or person; a universe of data; a universe of criteria; a universe of policies; and a decision sheet.)

_____ 14. Have I developed a decision sheet that each student can use to indicate his choice from among the policies listed, to state the relevant information (or good consequences) considered in the selection of his choice, and to identify the criterion by which he would argue in defense of his choice?

_____ 15. Have I considered and made provisions for small group discussions that frequently accompany this format of the value sheet? If so, have I prepared instructions for small group discussions?

_____ 16. Have I developed and written follow-up questions (discussion starters) that will assist students in sharing their understandings of the context—and of the features of the particular problem-solving situation—and in examining their decisions, preferences, and feelings?

_____ 17. Have I included questions designed to elicit student statements consistent with the comprehension, relational, and valuation phases of value clarification?

_____ 18. Have I secured enough copies of the value sheet and its decision sheet(s) for each student to read, study, and complete the components included in this value clarification activity?

_____ 19. Have I considered and made provisions for the preparation my students will need in order to use this value clarification activity?

_____ 20. Have I considered how I will make the transition from this activity in my instructional unit to the next activity I plan to use?

APPENDIX B

VERBAL CATEGORIES OF INQUIRY

The verbal approach to value clarification described in Chapter Two is derived from a model of class discussion. This model, called the Social Science Observation Record (SSOR), is designed to describe verbal interactions between students and their teacher. The system embraces ten categories of student statements, five categories of teacher statements, and two categories of nonverbal behavior. For ease of reference, these seventeen categories, and short definitions for each, are presented in the following table.

REALM	CATEGORY OF STATEMENT	SHORT DEFINITIONS
I. Subject-Centered	1. Topical	Student statements identifying the theme, unit, concept, issue, or problem on which group discussion is focused.
	2. Empirical	Student statements providing verifiable data from memory, observation, reading, or oral presentation.
	3. Interpretive	Student statements assigning meaning to data or experience and expressed as notions, opinions, comparisons, relationships, and connections.
	4. Defining	Student statements as to the meaning of a word or concept by reference to an accepted source, by context, by examples, by operant criteria, or by ideal type.
	5. Clarifying	Student statements rewording, rephrasing, elaborating on, or expanding on other statements by way of explanation.
II. Teacher-Centered	6. Infirming	Teacher or student statements of rejection, criticism, closure, or dissatisfaction expressed sarcastically, doctrinally, or negatively.
	7. Commentary	Teacher or student statements reviewing or summarizing the directions of a group; or, teacher statements summarizing, consolidating, structuring, providing new information, new directions, or responding to student requests for information.
	8. Dissonant	Teacher or student statements indicating that what is being said is not understood, is causing confusion, or lacks either internal or external consistency.
	9. Interrogative	Teacher or student questions expressed during group interaction.
	10. Confirming	Teacher or student statements expressing acceptance, satisfaction, encouragement, or praise.
III. Man-Centered	11. Preferential	Student statements assigning a value rating or classification to an idea, person, group, object, etc.
	12. Consequential	Student statements identifying the known or anticipated effects of an action, idea, object, feeling, etc.
	13. Criterial	Student statements identifying the basis for a decision, a judgment, an action, an interpretation, etc.; or, developing a table of specifications for use in decisionmaking.
	14. Imperative	Student statements of what should or should not be; of what ought or ought not to be done; or expressing a decision achieved by the group.
	15. Emotive	Student statements indicating personal feelings; or, efforts to express empathy, regarding the personal feelings of others.
IV. Non-Verbal	16. Silence	Period indicating quiet, absence of verbal interaction, reading, thinking, non-verbal activities, or work.
	17. Confusion	Verbal or non-verbal interference or commotion causing communication difficulties with the group.

Categories of the Social Science Observation Record (Source: Casteel and Stahl, 1972).